Algebra 1 (Florida's B.E.S.T Stand...

MW01489341

Unit 6 - Quadratic Func...

Unit 10 - Function Review		
Lesson	**Title**	**Pg #**
1	Comparing Linear, Quadratic, and Exponential	188
2	Parent Functions	195
3	Transformation of Functions	200
4	Interpret Equations and Expressions	206
5	Real World Functions	211
6	Average Rate of Change	216

Unit 6 - Quadratic Functions

Unit 6 Lesson 1: Key Features of a Quadratic Function Graph

MA.912.AR.3.7: Given a table, equation or written description of a quadratic function, graph that function, and determine and interpret its key features.

MA.912.AR.3.6: Given an expression or equation representing a quadratic function, determine the vertex and zeros and interpret them in terms of a real-world context.

SHOW US WHAT YOU KNOW!

1) Write the standard form equation for the table given.

x	-3	6	12
y	-8	-5	-3

Standard form:

BRAIN WORKOUT!

Formulas, Vocabulary, and/or any steps you've learned to solve problems in Algebra!

VOCABULARY

Function	For every input there is exactly one output. The x values cannot repeat!
Linear Function	A function that creates a straight line. Degree = Largest exponent on variable = 1 **1) Slope = Constant Rate of Change =** $$m = \frac{y_2 - y_1}{x_2 - x_1}$$ **2) Point-Slope Form:** $y - y_1 = m(x - x_1)$ **3) Slope-Intercept Form:** $y = mx + b$ **4) Standard Form:** $Ax + By = C$
Quadratic Function	A function that creates a parabola. Degree = Largest exponent on variable = 2 **1) Standard Form:** $$y = ax^2 + bx \boxed{+ c}$$ Y-intercept / Initial value

To find vertex:

To Find Vertex:	
Axis of symmetry: $x = h = \frac{-b}{2a}$	**Plug in x to get y=k** **This is your range**

2) Quadratic Formula:
$$x = \frac{-b \pm \sqrt{b^2 - 4ac}}{2a} = p \text{ and } q$$
3) Vertex Form: $y = a(x - h)^2 + k$
    (h, k) = Vertex
4) Factored Form: $y = a(x - p)(x - q)$
    p and q represent x-intercepts

To Find Vertex:	
Axis of symmetry: $x = h = \frac{p+q}{2}$	**Plug in x to get y=k** **This is your range**

X-INTERCEPT	$(x, 0)$ Plug 0 into y
Y-INTERCEPT	$(0, y)$ Plug 0 into x
DOMAIN X	Set of inputs in the function. The independent variable. Time
RANGE Y=f(x)	Set of outputs in the function. The dependent variable. Total once you input x value.
VIABLE	The inputs and outputs satisfy the functions constraints.
NON -VIABLE	The inputs and outputs DO NOT satisfy the functions constraints.

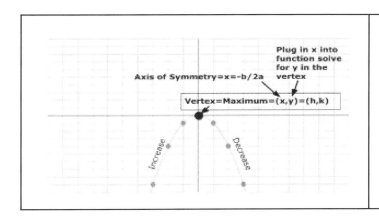

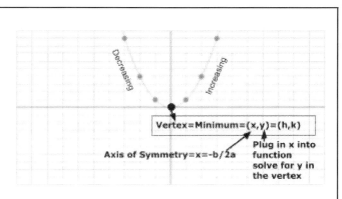

Find the key features of the graph, then label the graph.

EXAMPLE: $y = x^2$

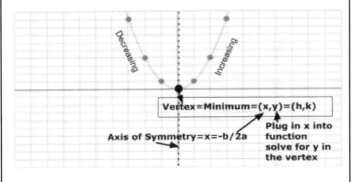

$a: 1$	$b: 0$	$c: 0$

Maximum/Minimum:	Minimum=0
Vertex:	(0,0)
Axis of Symmetry:	x=0
$x - intercept(s):$ $root(s):$ $zero(s):$	One Solution= (0,0)
$y - intercept:$	(0,0)
Domain:	$-\infty \leq x \leq \infty$
Range:	$y \geq 0$
Increasing Interval:	$x > 0$
Decreasing Interval:	$x < 0$
$As\ x \rightarrow \infty$	$y \rightarrow \infty$
$As\ x \rightarrow -\infty$	$y \rightarrow \infty$

1) 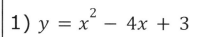 $y = x^2 - 4x + 3$

a:	b:	c:

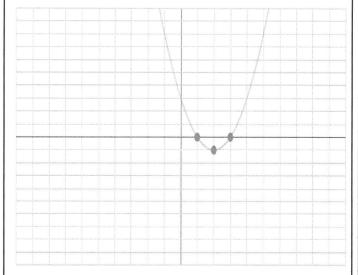

Maximum/Minimum:	
Vertex:	
Axis of Symmetry:	
x − intercept(s): *root(s):* *zero(s):*	
y − intercept:	
Domain:	
Range:	
Increasing Interval:	
Decreasing Interval:	
As x → ∞	*y →*
As x → − ∞	*y →*

2) $y = -x^2 - 6x - 12$

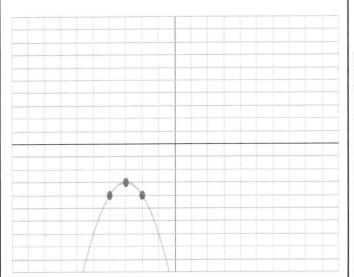

a:	b:	c:

Maximum/Minimum:	
Vertex:	
Axis of Symmetry:	
$x - intercept(s)$: $root(s)$: $zero(s)$:	
$y - intercept$:	
Domain:	
Range:	
Increasing Interval:	
Decreasing Interval:	
As $x \rightarrow \infty$	$y \rightarrow$
As $x \rightarrow -\infty$	$y \rightarrow$

3) $y = -\frac{3}{4}(x + 2)(x - 2)$

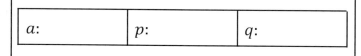

a:	p:	q:

Maximum/Minimum:	
Vertex:	
Axis of Symmetry:	
$x - intercept(s):$ $root(s):$ $zero(s):$	
$y - intercept:$	
Domain:	
Range:	
Increasing Interval:	
Decreasing Interval:	
As $x \to \infty$	$y \to$
As $x \to -\infty$	$y \to$

4) $y = 2(x + 4)^2 - 3$

a:	h:	k:

Maximum/Minimum:	
Vertex:	
Axis of Symmetry:	
Approximate $x - intercept(s)$: $root(s)$: $zero(s)$:	
$y - intercept$:	
Domain:	
Range:	
Increasing Interval:	
Decreasing Interval:	
As $x \to \infty$	$y \to$
As $x \to -\infty$	$y \to$

 TEST TIME!

1) Select all of the key features of the Quadratic Function.

- [ ] $(2, -5)$ *is a viable solution*
- [ ] *No roots*
- [ ] $(-5, 0)$ *is a viable solution*
- [ ] $y - intercept\ is\ -5$
- [ ] $Vertex\ = (1, -3)$
- [ ] $Axis\ of\ symmetry\ is\ x\ = -3$
- [ ] $As\ x \rightarrow \infty,\ y \rightarrow \infty$
- [ ] $As\ x \rightarrow \infty,\ y \rightarrow -\infty$
- [ ] $As\ x \rightarrow -\infty,\ y \rightarrow \infty$
- [ ] $As\ x \rightarrow -\infty,\ y \rightarrow -\infty$

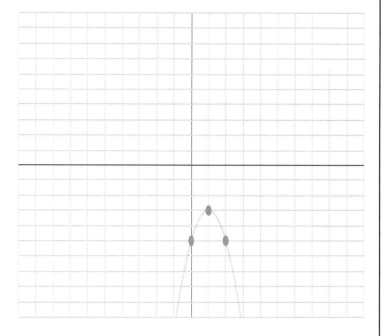

Unit 6 Lesson 2: Standard Form-Key Features

MA.912.AR.1.2:Rearrange equations or formulas to isolate a quantity of interest.

MA.912.AR.3.7:Given a table, equation or written description of a quadratic function, graph that function, and determine and interpret its key features.

MA.912.AR.3.6:Given an expression or equation representing a quadratic function, determine the vertex and zeros and interpret them in terms of a real-world context.

 SHOW US WHAT YOU KNOW!

1) **Factor** the binomial expression.

$3x^4 - 147x^2$

Check:

BRAIN WORKOUT!
STEPS OF A QUADRATIC:

KEY FEATURES OF A STANDARD FORM QUADRATIC FUNCTION

Standard Form:

$y = ax^2 + bx + c$

Example: $y = x^2 + 2x - 3$

1) Label a, b, c **a=1 b=2 c=-3**	2) Find Axis of Symmetry: $x = -\frac{b}{2a} =$ $\frac{-2}{2(1)} = \frac{-2}{2} = -1$ $x = -1$	3) Input x into the function to solve for y(max/min): Follow Order of operations!!! $y = x^2 + 2x - 3$ $y = (-1)^2 + 2(-1) - 3$ $y = 1 + 2(-1) - 3$ $y = 1 - 2 - 3$ $y = -4 = Minimum$
4)Vertex=(h,k): **(-1,-4)**	5) x-intercept(s)=get 0 for y! If b=0 solve for x. If $b \neq 0$ use the quadratic formula! $x = \frac{-b \pm \sqrt{b^2 - 4ac}}{2a} = p \ and \ q$ **(1,0) and (-3,0)**	6) y-intercept=c: **(0,-3)**
7) Domain= x values: $-\infty \leq x \leq \infty$	8) Range= y values: <table><tr><td>a=+ $y \geq k$</td><td>a=- $y \leq k$</td></tr></table> $y \geq -4$	9) Increasing/Decreasing Interval a=+ $As \ x \to \infty, \ y \to \infty$ $As \ x \to -\infty, \ y \to \infty$ a=- $As \ x \to \infty, \ y \to -\infty$ $As \ x \to \infty, \ y \to -\infty$ **Increasing: x>-1** **Decreasing: x<-1** $As \ x \to \infty, \ y \to \infty$ $As \ x \to -\infty, \ y \to \infty$

Write down the key features of the equation given.

1) $y = x^2$ (PARENT FUNCTION)

a:	b:	c:

Maximum/Minimum:

Axis of Symmetry:	
Vertex:	
$y - intercept$:	
Domain:	
Range:	
Increasing Interval:	
Decreasing Interval:	
As $x \to \infty$	$y \to$
As $x \to -\infty$	$y \to$

2) $y = -x^2 - 8$

a:	b:	c:

Maximum/Minimum:

Axis of Symmetry:	
Vertex:	
$y - intercept$:	
Domain:	
Range:	
Increasing Interval:	
Decreasing Interval:	
As $x \to \infty$	$y \to$
As $x \to -\infty$	$y \to$

3) $f(x) = -\frac{1}{2}x^2 - 7x + 12$

a:	b:	c:

Maximum/Minimum:

Axis of Symmetry:	
Vertex:	
y − intercept:	
Domain:	
Range:	
Increasing Interval:	
Decreasing Interval:	
As x → ∞	y →
As x → − ∞	y →

4) $y = 2x^2 + 4x - 26$

a:	b:	c:

Maximum/Minimum:

Axis of Symmetry:	
Vertex:	
y − intercept:	
Domain:	
Range:	
Increasing Interval:	
Decreasing Interval:	
As x → ∞	y →
As x → − ∞	y →

TEST TIME!

1) Select all of the key features of the quadratic function.

$$7x - 3 = -\frac{1}{2}x^2 + 3x + 3$$

☐ *The y − intercept is* 6

☐ *The y − intercept is* $- 4$

☐ *Vertex* $= (- 4, 14)$

☐ *Axis of symmetry is* $x = - 4$

☐ *As $x \to \infty$, $y \to \infty$*

☐ *As $x \to \infty$, $y \to - \infty$*

Unit 6 Lesson 3: Solving Quadratic Equations Using Square Roots

MA.912.AR.1.2: Rearrange equations or formulas to isolate a quantity of interest.

MA.912.AR.9.6: Given a real-world context, represent constraints as systems of linear equations or inequalities. Interpret solutions to problems as viable or non-viable options.

MA.912.AR.3.1: Given a mathematical or real-world context, write and solve one-variable quadratic equations over the real number system.

 SHOW US WHAT YOU KNOW!

1) Select all of the viable solutions to the inequality:

$$\frac{1}{2}x - 6y \geq 24$$

☐ (0,1)

☐ (4,4)

☐ (4,-4)

☐ (0,-4)

☐ (8,2)

BRAIN WORKOUT!
STEPS OF A QUADRATIC:

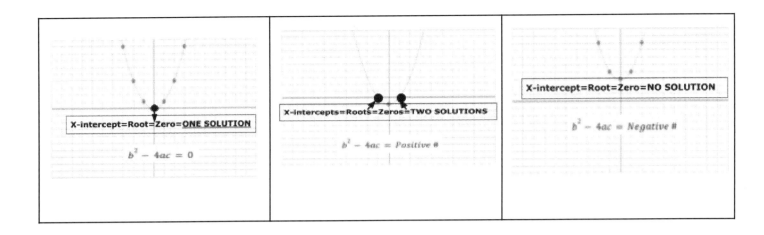

X-intercept=Root=Zero=**ONE SOLUTION**

$b^2 - 4ac = 0$

X-intercepts=Roots=Zeros=**TWO SOLUTIONS**

$b^2 - 4ac = Positive \#$

X-intercept=Root=Zero=**NO SOLUTION**

$b^2 - 4ac = Negative \#$

STEPS TO SOLVING THE X-INTERCEPTS USING SQUARE ROOTS

GOAL: Solve for the zeros, roots, x-intercept(s) of the Quadratic Function.

* This method could ONLY be used if b=0 in the standard form equation

$y = ax^2 + bx + c$

1.	To find the x-intercept(s) the y must equal 0. Set y equal to 0.
2.	Label a, b, and c. MAKE SURE b=0!!!
3.	Use your properties to isolate x!!! If the equation equals a numerical value, isolate the x to solve for the intercept(s).
4.	Solve for X: Use the **Addition/Subtraction Property of Equality, the Multiplication Property of Equality/Division Property of Equality,**
5.	Square Root both sides of the equation. MAKE SURE TO MAKE IT A POSITIVE AND NEGATIVE. You now have your x-intercept(s) of the graph!!!!

Find the solution(s)/root(s)/zero(s) to each Quadratic Function.

1) $y = x^2 - 16$ a: b: c:	2) $y = x^2 + 25$ a: b: c:
3) $2x^2 - 65 = -65$ a: b: c:	4) $\frac{1}{2}x^2 + 4 = 2$ a: b: c:
5) $y = x^2 - 9$ a: b: c:	6) $\frac{-1}{2}(x^2 - 4) + x^2 = 34$ a: b: c:

7) $y = \frac{3}{5}x^2 + 7$

a:	b:	c:

8) $x^2 + 81 = 7$

a:	b:	c:

9) $t^2 = 144$

a:	b:	c:

10) $3z^2 - 18 = 489$

a:	b:	c:

TEST TIME!

1) Select all of the solutions to the Quadratic Function:

$$y = x^2 - \frac{4}{25}$$

☐ $x = \frac{4}{25}$

☐ $x = \frac{-4}{25}$

☐ *The roots to the equation are* $x = \frac{2}{5}$ *and* $x = \frac{-2}{5}$

☐ $x = 0$

☐ *The zeros of the Function are are* $x = \frac{2}{5}$ *and* $x = \frac{-2}{5}$

☐ *The* $x -$ *intercepts of the equation are* $(\frac{2}{5}, 0)$ *and* $(\frac{-2}{5}, 0)$

Unit 6 Lesson 4: Solving Quadratic Equations Using Quadratic Formula

MA.912.AR.1.2: Rearrange equations or formulas to isolate a quantity of interest.

MA.912.AR.9.6: Given a real-world context, represent constraints as systems of linear equations or inequalities. Interpret solutions to problems as viable or non-viable options.

MA.912.AR.3.1: Given a mathematical or real-world context, write and solve one-variable quadratic equations over the real number system.

 SHOW US WHAT YOU KNOW!

1)Graph $f(x) = \frac{1}{2}x + 4$

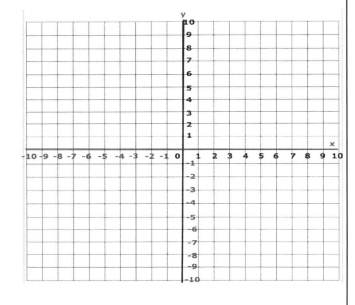

BRAIN WORKOUT!
STEPS OF A QUADRATIC:

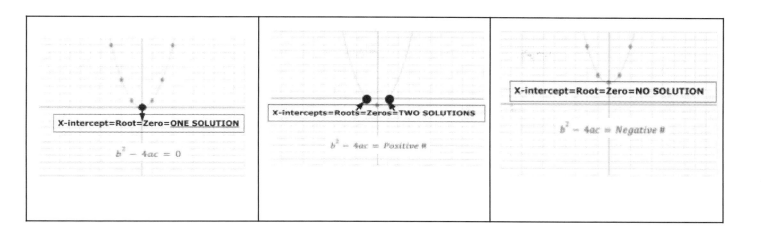

X-intercept=Root=Zero=ONE SOLUTION
$b^2 - 4ac = 0$

X-intercepts=Roots=Zeros=TWO SOLUTIONS
$b^2 - 4ac = Positive\ \#$

X-intercept=Root=Zero=NO SOLUTION
$b^2 - 4ac = Negative\ \#$

STEPS TO SOLVING THE X-INTERCEPTS USING THE QUADRATIC FORMULA

GOAL: Solve for the zeros, roots, x-intercept(s), solutions, ground of the Quadratic Function.

* This method could ONLY be used if y=0 and it is in standard form!

$$0 = ax^2 + bx + c$$

3.	Set y equal to 0.
4.	Label a, b, and c.
3.	Find the Discriminant: $$b^2 - 4ac$$
4.	Plug a, b, and c and the discriminant into the **Quadratic Formula:** $$x = \frac{-b \pm \sqrt{b^2 - 4ac}}{2a} \longleftarrow \text{Discriminant}$$
5.	Square root the discriminant: $$\sqrt{Discriminant} = b^2 - 4ac$$
6.	Write 2 equations and solve: $$x = \frac{-b + \sqrt{b^2 - 4ac}}{2a} \quad and \quad x = \frac{-b - \sqrt{b^2 - 4ac}}{2a}$$

Solve the Quadratic Function using the quadratic formula. Write down the Key Features of the graph.

1) $y = 6x^2 - 12x + 7$

a:	b:	c:

$x - intercept(s)$:		

Axis of Symmetry:	
Vertex:	
$y - intercept$:	
Increasing Interval:	
Decreasing Interval:	
As $x \to \infty$	$y \to$
As $x \to -\infty$	$y \to$

2) $-6x^2 = -5x^2 - 20x - 3$

a:	b:	c:

$x - intercept(s)$:		

Axis of Symmetry:	
Vertex:	
$y - intercept$:	
Increasing Interval:	
Decreasing Interval:	
As $x \to \infty$	$y \to$
As $x \to -\infty$	$y \to$

3) $-x^2 + 20x - 25 = 10x$

a:	b:	c:

$x - intercept(s)$:		

Axis of Symmetry:	
Vertex:	
$y - intercept$:	
Increasing Interval:	
Decreasing Interval:	
As $x \to \infty$	$y \to$
As $x \to -\infty$	$y \to$

4) $2b^2 - 4 = 28$

a:	b:	c:

$x - intercept(s)$:		

Axis of Symmetry:	
Vertex:	
$y - intercept$:	
Increasing Interval:	
Decreasing Interval:	
As $x \to \infty$	$y \to$
As $x \to -\infty$	$y \to$

TEST TIME!

1) Select all of the solutions to the Quadratic Function:

$$-2 = 9x^2 + 54x + 8$$

☐ $x = -2$

☐ *The roots are* $-3 \pm \frac{1}{3}\sqrt{71}$

☐ *The roots to the equation are* $x = \frac{2}{5}$ *and* $x = \frac{-2}{5}$

☐ $x = -3 + \frac{1}{3}\sqrt{71}$

☐ $x = -3 - \frac{1}{3}\sqrt{71}$

Unit 6 Lesson 5: Factored Form- Key Features

MA.912.AR.1.2: Rearrange equations or formulas to isolate a quantity of interest.

MA.912.AR.3.7: Given a table, equation or written description of a quadratic function, graph that function, and determine and interpret its key features.

MA.912.AR.3.6: Given an expression or equation representing a quadratic function, determine the vertex and zeros and interpret them in terms of a real-world context.

 SHOW US WHAT YOU KNOW!

1) Write the equation in standard form for the line that is perpendicular to y=2x+7 and passes through the point (-1,8).

Standard form:

BRAIN WORKOUT!
STEPS OF A LINE:

PARALLEL:

PERPENDICULAR:

DOMAIN:

RANGE:

X-INTERCEPT:

Y-INTERCEPT:

KEY FEATURES OF A FACTORED FORM QUADRATIC FUNCTION

Factored Form:

$y = a(x - p)(x - q)$

Example: $y = -(x - 5)(x + 3)$
1) Label a
a=-1
2) Label p and q
p=5
q=-3
3) Find Vertex:

axis of symmetry:	Plug in axis of symmetry to find y in vertex:
$x = \frac{p+q}{2}$	$y = -(1 - 5)(1 + 3)$
$x = \frac{5+-3}{2}$	$y = -(-4)(4)$
$x = 1$	$y = -(-16)$
	$y = -16$

(1,-16)
4) Maximum/Minimum

Maximum	Minimum
a=-	a=+
k value	k value

$Maximum = -16$
5) Domain= x values:
$-\infty \leq x \leq \infty$
6) Range= y values:

a=+	a=-
$y \geq k$	$y \leq k$

$y \leq -16$
7) Increasing/Decreasing Interval

a=+	a=-
$As\ x \to \infty,\ y \to \infty$	$As\ x \to \infty,\ y \to -\infty$
$As\ x \to -\infty,\ y \to \infty$	$As\ x \to -\infty,\ y \to -\infty$

Increasing: x<1   **Decreasing: x>1**
$As\ x \to \infty,\ y \to -\infty$
$As\ x \to -\infty,\ y \to -\infty$

Write down the key features of the Equation given.

1) $y = -\frac{1}{2}(x - 8)(x - 4)$

a:	p:	q:

Axis of symmetry work:	y in the vertex work:
Axis of symmetry:	Vertex:
x-intercept work:	y-intercept work:
x-intercept(s):	y-intercept:

Maximum/Minimum:	
Domain:	
Range:	
As $x \to \infty$	$y \to$
As $x \to -\infty$	$y \to$

2) $y = 2(x + 13)(x - 1)$

a:	p:	q:

Axis of symmetry work:	y in the vertex work:
Axis of symmetry:	Vertex:
x-intercept work:	y-intercept work:
x-intercept(s):	y-intercept:

Maximum/Minimum:	
Domain:	
Range:	
As $x \to \infty$	$y \to$
As $x \to -\infty$	$y \to$

3) $y = -(4x - 8)(2x - 3)$

a:	p:	q:

Axis of symmetry work:	y in the vertex work:
Axis of symmetry:	Vertex:
x-intercept work:	y-intercept work:
x-intercept(s):	y-intercept:

Maximum/Minimum:	
Domain:	
Range:	
As x $\to \infty$	*y* $\to$
As x $\to -\infty$	*y* $\to$

4) $y = 5(x + 7)(11x - 33)$

a:	p:	q:

Axis of symmetry work:	y in the vertex work:
Axis of symmetry:	Vertex:
x-intercept work:	y-intercept work:
x-intercept(s):	y-intercept:

Maximum/Minimum:	
Domain:	
Range:	
As x $\to \infty$	*y* $\to$
As x $\to -\infty$	*y* $\to$

 **TEST TIME!**

1) Select all of the key features of the quadratic function.

$$y = 2(4x + 2)(x - 1)$$

☐ $(0, -4)$ $is\ the\ y - intercept$

☐ $\frac{-1}{2}$ $is\ a\ solution\ to\ the\ quadratic\ equation$

☐ $Vertex\ = (\frac{-9}{2}, \frac{1}{4})$

☐ $Axis\ of\ symmetry\ is\ x\ = \frac{1}{4}$

☐ $As\ x \to \infty,\ y \to \infty$

☐ $As\ x \to \infty,\ y \to -\infty$

☐ $As\ x \to -\infty,\ y \to \infty$

☐ $As\ x \to -\infty,\ y \to -\infty$

Unit 6 Lesson 6: Solving Quadratic Equations Using Factoring

MA.912.AR.1.2:Rearrange equations or formulas to isolate a quantity of interest.

MA.912.AR.9.6:Given a real-world context, represent constraints as systems of linear equations or inequalities. Interpret solutions to problems as viable or non-viable options.

MA.912.AR.3.1:Given a mathematical or real-world context, write and solve one-variable quadratic equations over the real number system.

 SHOW US WHAT YOU KNOW!

1)Select all of the viable solutions to the Quadratic Function:

$$y = 4x^2 - 12x + 8$$

☐ (0,1)

☐ (1,0)

☐ (2,0)

☐ (0,2)

☐ (-1,0)

☐ (0,-1)

BRAIN WORKOUT!
STEPS OF A LINE:

PARALLEL:

PERPENDICULAR:

DOMAIN:

RANGE:

X-INTERCEPT:

Y-INTERCEPT:

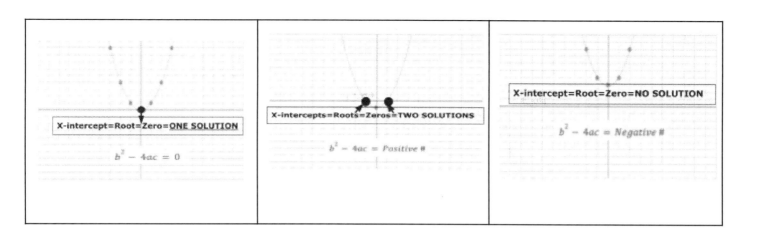

STEPS TO SOLVING THE X-INTERCEPTS USING FACTORING

GOAL: Solve for the zeros, roots, x-intercept(s), solutions, ground of the Quadratic Function.
* This method could ONLY be used if the function can be factored.

5.	Set y equal to 0.
6.	Label a, b, and c.
3.	Factor the trinomial by grouping.
4.	Set each factor equal to 0.
5.	Solve for X: Use the Addition/Subtraction Property of Equality, and the Multiplication Property of Equality/Division Property of Equality.

Solve the Quadratic Function. Write the Factored Form of the function. Write down the key features of the graph.

1) $y = x^2 + 2x + 1$

a:	b:	c:

Factored Form:

$x - intercept(s)$:		

Axis of Symmetry:	
Vertex:	
$y - intercept$:	
Increasing Interval:	
Decreasing Interval:	
As $x \to \infty$	$y \to$
As $x \to -\infty$	$y \to$

2) $3x^2 - 5x - 6 = 2x^2 - 12$

a:	b:	c:

Factored Form:

$x - intercept(s)$:		

Axis of Symmetry:	
Vertex:	
$y - intercept$:	
Increasing Interval:	
Decreasing Interval:	
As $x \to \infty$	$y \to$
As $x \to -\infty$	$y \to$

3) $2b^2 + 4b - 16 = 8b$

a:	b:	c:

Factored Form:

$x - intercept(s)$:		

$Axis\ of\ Symmetry$:	
$Vertex$:	
$y - intercept$:	
$Increasing$ $Interval$:	
$Decreasing$ $Interval$:	
$As\ x \to \infty$	$y \to$
$As\ x \to -\infty$	$y \to$

4) $y = -2x^2 - 2x + 24$

a:	b:	c:

Factored Form:

$x - intercept(s)$:		

$Axis\ of\ Symmetry$:	
$Vertex$:	
$y - intercept$:	
$Increasing$ $Interval$:	
$Decreasing$ $Interval$:	
$As\ x \to \infty$	$y \to$
$As\ x \to -\infty$	$y \to$

TEST TIME!

1) Select all of the solutions to the Quadratic Function:

$$y = 4x^2 - 12x + 8$$

☐ $(1, 0)$

☐ $(0, 1)$

☐ *The roots to the equation is no real solution*

☐ $(2, 0)$

☐ $(0, 2)$

Unit 6 Lesson 7: Vertex Form- Key Features

MA.912.AR.1.2: Rearrange equations or formulas to isolate a quantity of interest.

MA.912.AR.3.7: Given a table, equation or written description of a quadratic function, graph that function, and determine and interpret its key features.

MA.912.AR.3.6: Given an expression or equation representing a quadratic function, determine the vertex and zeros and interpret them in terms of a real-world context.

 SHOW US WHAT YOU KNOW!

1) Write the equation in standard form for the line that is parallel to $y=2x+7$ and passes through the point (-1,8).

Standard form:

BRAIN WORKOUT!
STEPS OF A QUADRATIC:

KEY FEATURES OF A VERTEX FORM QUADRATIC FUNCTION

Vertex Form:

$y = a(x - h)^2 + k$

Example: $y = -(x - 5)^2 - 8$

1) Label a

a=-1

2)Vertex=(h,k):

(5,-8)

3) Maximum/Minimum

Maximum	Minimum
a=-	a=+
k value	k value

$Maximum = -8$

4)Domain= x values:

$-\infty \leq x \leq \infty$

5) Range= y values:

a=+	a=-
$y \geq k$	$y \leq k$

$y \leq -8$

6) Increasing/Decreasing Interval

a=+	a=-
$As\ x \to \infty, y \to \infty$	$As\ x \to \infty, y \to -\infty$
$As\ x \to -\infty, y \to \infty$	$As\ x \to -\infty, y \to -\infty$

Increasing: x<5

Decreasing: x>5

$As\ x \to \infty, y \to -\infty$

$As\ x \to -\infty, y \to -\infty$

Write down the key features of the Equation given.

1) $y = -2(x-3)^2 + 8$

a:	h:	k:

x-intercept work:	y-intercept work:

Axis of Symmetry:	
Maximum/Minimum:	
Vertex:	
x − intercept:	
y − intercept:	
Domain:	
Range:	
Increasing Interval:	
Decreasing Interval:	
As x → ∞	y →
As x → − ∞	y →

2) $y = (x+5)^2 + 6$

a:	h:	k:

x-intercept work:	y-intercept work:

Axis of Symmetry:	
Maximum/Minimum:	
Vertex:	
x − intercept:	
y − intercept:	
Domain:	
Range:	
Increasing Interval:	
Decreasing Interval:	
As x → ∞	y →
As x → − ∞	y →

3) $y = -(x-8)^2 - 1$

a:	h:	k:

x-intercept work:	y-intercept work:

Axis of Symmetry:	
Maximum/Minimum:	
Vertex:	
x − intercept:	
y − intercept:	
Domain:	
Range:	
Increasing Interval:	
Decreasing Interval:	
As $x \to \infty$	$y \to$
As $x \to -\infty$	$y \to$

4) $y = \frac{1}{2}(x+1)^2 - 6$

a:	h:	k:

x-intercept work:	y-intercept work:

Axis of Symmetry:	
Maximum/Minimum:	
Vertex:	
x − intercept:	
y − intercept:	
Domain:	
Range:	
Increasing Interval:	
Decreasing Interval:	
As $x \to \infty$	$y \to$
As $x \to -\infty$	$y \to$

TEST TIME!

1) Select all of the key features of the quadratic function.

$$y - 10 = -\frac{1}{2}(x - 4)^2 + 6$$

☐ $(8, 0)$ *is the* $y - intercept$

☐ $y - intercept$ *is* 6

☐ $Vertex = (4, 16)$

☐ $Vertex = (4, 6)$

☐ $Axis\ of\ symmetry\ is\ x = 4$

☐ $As\ x \to \infty,\ y\ decreases$

☐ $As\ x \to -\infty,\ y\ increases$

☐ $As\ x \to -\infty,\ y\ decreases$

Unit 6 Lesson 8: Writing Different Forms of a Quadratic Function

MA.912.AR.1.2: Rearrange equations or formulas to isolate a quantity of interest.

MA.912.AR.3.7: Given a table, equation or written description of a quadratic function, graph that function, and determine and interpret its key features.

MA.912.AR.3.6: Given an expression or equation representing a quadratic function, determine the vertex and zeros and interpret them in terms of a real-world context.

 SHOW US WHAT YOU KNOW!

1) Factor $7x^2 + 26x - 8$

BRAIN WORKOUT!
STEPS OF A QUADRATIC:

Change the form of each Quadratic Function. Find the key features.

1) EXAMPLE: $y = x^2 - 6x + 2$

$a: 1$	$b: -6$	$c: 2$

Work for vertex:	Work for x-intercept(s)/root(s)/zero(s):
1) FIND AXIS OF SYMMETRY: $x = \frac{-b}{2a} = \frac{6}{2(1)} = \frac{6}{2} = 3$ $x = 3 = h$ 2) Input x into the function to solve for y: $y = x^2 - 6x + 2$ $y = (3)^2 - 6(3) + 2$ $y = 9 - 18 + 2$ $y = -7 = k$ 3) Plug in a, h, k into vertex form:	$x = \frac{6 \pm \sqrt{(-6^2)-4(1)(2)}}{2(1)}$ $x = \frac{6 \pm \sqrt{36-8}}{2}$ $x = \frac{6 \pm \sqrt{28}}{2}$ $x = \frac{6 \pm 2\sqrt{7}}{2}$ $x = 3 \pm 2\sqrt{7}$

Vertex Form: $y = 1(x - 3)^2 - 7$

Axis of Symmetry:	x=3	$x - intercept(s)/$ $root(s)/$ $zero(s)$	☐ $x = 3 \pm 2\sqrt{7}$
Vertex:	(3,-7)	$y - intercept$:	☐ (0,2)
Increasing Interval:	x>3	Decreasing Interval:	☐ x<3
As x increases, y:	☑ Increases ☐ Decreases	As x decreases, y:	☑ Increases ☐ Decreases
Domain:	$-\infty \leq x \leq \infty$	Range:	☐ $-7 \leq y \leq \infty$

2) $y = -x^2 - 4x - 4$

a:	b:	c:

Work for vertex:	Work for x-intercept(s)/root(s)/zero(s):

Vertex Form:

Axis of Symmetry:		$x - intercept(s)/$ $root(s)/$ $zero(s)$	
Vertex:		$y - intercept$:	
Increasing Interval:		Decreasing Interval:	
As x increases, y:	☐ Increases ☐ Decreases	As x decreases, y:	☐ Increases ☐ Decreases
Domain:		Range:	

3) $y = (x + 7)(x - 5)$

a:	p:	q:

Work for vertex:	Work for standard form:

Standard Form:

Axis of Symmetry:		$x - intercept(s)/$ $root(s)/$ $zero(s)$	
Vertex:		$y - intercept$:	
Increasing Interval:		*Decreasing Interval*:	
As x increases, y:	☐ *Increases* ☐ *Decreases*	*As x decreases, y*:	☐ *Increases* ☐ *Decreases*
Domain:		*Range*:	

4) $y = -(x + 3)(x - 9)$

a:	p:	q:

Work for vertex:	Work for standard form:

Standard Form:

Axis of Symmetry:		$x - intercept(s)/$ $root(s)/$ $zero(s)$	
Vertex:		$y - intercept$:	
Increasing Interval:		Decreasing Interval:	
As x increases, y:	☐ Increases ☐ Decreases	As x decreases, y:	☐ Increases ☐ Decreases
Domain:		Range:	

5) $y = -2(x + 4)^2 - 3$

a:	h:	k:

Work for standard form:	Work for x-intercept(s)/root(s)/zero(s):

Standard Form:

Axis of Symmetry:		$x - intercept(s)/$ $root(s)/$ $zero(s)$	
Vertex:		$y - intercept$:	
Increasing Interval:		Decreasing Interval:	
As x increases, y:	☐ Increases ☐ Decreases	As x decreases, y:	☐ Increases ☐ Decreases
Domain:		Range:	

6) $y = -(x - 5)^2$

a:	h:	k:

Work for standard form:	Work for x-intercept(s)/root(s)/zero(s):

Standard Form:

Axis of Symmetry:		$x - intercept(s)/$ $root(s)/$ $zero(s)$	
Vertex:		$y - intercept:$	
Increasing Interval:		Decreasing Interval:	
As x increases, y:	☐ Increases ☐ Decreases	As x decreases, y:	☐ Increases ☐ Decreases
Domain:		Range:	

1) Write the Factored Form in Standard Form and Vertex Form.

$$y = -(x + 4)(x - 2)$$

Standard Form:	Vertex Form:

Unit 6 Lesson 9: Graphing Key Features of Quadratic Equations

MA.912.AR.1.2: Rearrange equations or formulas to isolate a quantity of interest.

MA.912.AR.3.7: Given a table, equation or written description of a quadratic function, graph that function, and determine and interpret its key features.

MA.912.AR.3.6: Given an expression or equation representing a quadratic function, determine the vertex and zeros and interpret them in terms of a real-world context.

 SHOW US WHAT YOU KNOW!

1) Factor $- 6x^2 + x + 35$

BRAIN WORKOUT!
STEPS OF A QUADRATIC:

Graph each quadratic function and write the key features of the graph.

1) $y = x^2 - 6x + 1$

a:	b:	c:

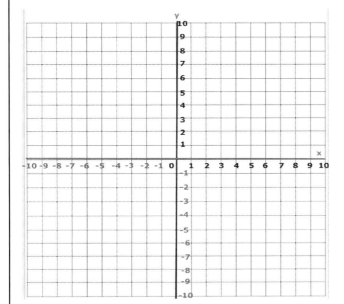

Axis of Symmetry:	
Vertex:	
$y - intercept$:	
Increasing Interval:	
Decreasing Interval:	
As $x \to \infty$	$y \to$
As $x \to -\infty$	$y \to$
Domain:	Range:

2) $y = -\frac{1}{2}x^2 - 4x - 1$

a:	b:	c:

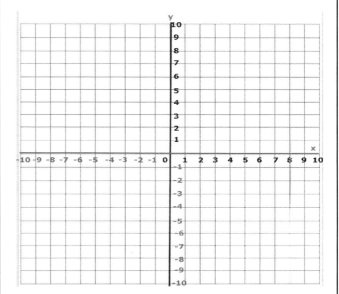

Axis of Symmetry:	
Vertex:	
$y - intercept$:	
Increasing Interval:	
Decreasing Interval:	
As $x \to \infty$	$y \to$
As $x \to -\infty$	$y \to$
Domain:	Range:

3) $y = (x + 5)(x - 3)$

a:	p:	q:

Standard Form:

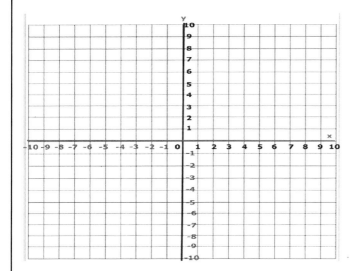

Axis of Symmetry:	
Vertex:	
$y - intercept$:	
$x - intercepts$: roots: zeros:	
As $x \to \infty$	$y \to$
As $x \to -\infty$	$y \to$
Domain:	Range:

4) $y = -(x - 4)(x - 2)$

a:	p:	q:

Standard Form:

Axis of Symmetry:	
Vertex:	
$y - intercept$:	
$x - intercepts$: roots: zeros:	
As $x \to \infty$	$y \to$
As $x \to -\infty$	$y \to$
Domain:	Range:

5) $y = -2(x + 4)^2 - 3$

a:	h:	k:

Standard Form:

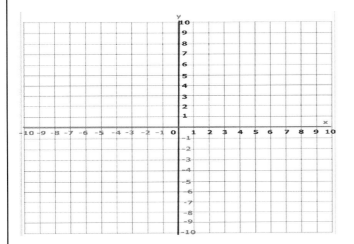

Vertex:	
Axis of Symmetry:	
$y - intercept$:	
Increasing Interval:	
Decreasing Interval:	
As $x \to \infty$	$y \to$
As $x \to -\infty$	$y \to$
Domain:	Range:

6) $y = -(x - 5)^2 + 4$

a:	h:	k:

Standard Form:

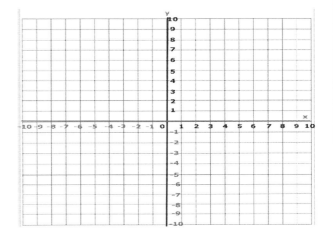

Vertex:	
Axis of Symmetry:	
$y - intercept$:	
Increasing Interval:	
Decreasing Interval:	
As $x \to \infty$	$y \to$
As $x \to -\infty$	$y \to$
Domain:	Range:

TEST TIME!

1) Graph the Quadratic Function.

$$y = -\frac{5}{2}x^2 - 5x + 5$$

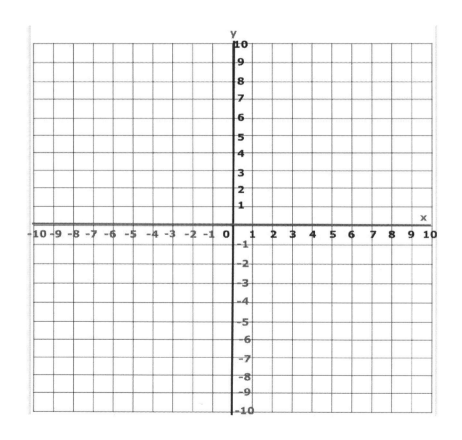

Unit 6 Lesson 10: Graphing Key Features of Quadratic Equations Given a Table

MA.912.AR.1.2: Rearrange equations or formulas to isolate a quantity of interest.

MA.912.AR.3.7: Given a table, equation or written description of a quadratic function, graph that function, and determine and interpret its key features.

MA.912.AR.3.6: Given an expression or equation representing a quadratic function, determine the vertex and zeros and interpret them in terms of a real-world context.

 SHOW US WHAT YOU KNOW!

1) Factor $2x^4 - 72x^2$

BRAIN WORKOUT!
STEPS OF A LINE:

PARALLEL:

PERPENDICULAR:

DOMAIN:

RANGE:

X-INTERCEPT:

Y-INTERCEPT:

Use the table to graph the function. Write the key features of the graph.

1)

x	$f(x) = x^2 - 4x + 5$	$f(x)$

Axis of Symmetry:	
Vertex:	
$y - intercept$:	
$x - intercept(s)$:	
Increasing Interval:	
Decreasing Interval:	
As $x \to \infty$	$y \to$
As $x \to -\infty$	$y \to$

2)

x	$y = -\frac{5}{2}x^2 - 5x - 2$	y

Axis of Symmetry:	
Vertex:	
$y - intercept$:	
$x - intercept(s)$:	
Increasing Interval:	
Decreasing Interval:	
As $x \to \infty$	$y \to$
As $x \to -\infty$	$y \to$

3)

x	$f(x) = -\frac{3}{5}(x-5)^2 + 7$	$f(x)$

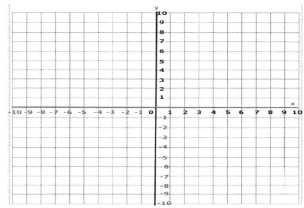

Axis of Symmetry:	
Vertex:	
$y-intercept$:	
$x-intercept(s)$:	
Increasing Interval:	
Decreasing Interval:	
As $x \to \infty$	$y \to$
As $x \to -\infty$	$y \to$

4)

x	$y = (x-1)(x+3)$	y

Axis of Symmetry:	
Vertex:	
$y-intercept$:	
$x-intercept(s)$:	
Increasing Interval:	
Decreasing Interval:	
As $x \to \infty$	$y \to$
As $x \to -\infty$	$y \to$

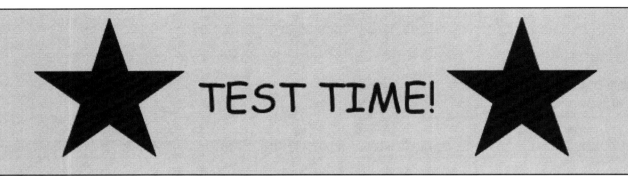

TEST TIME!

1) Graph the Quadratic Function.

$$y = 6x^2 + 12x$$

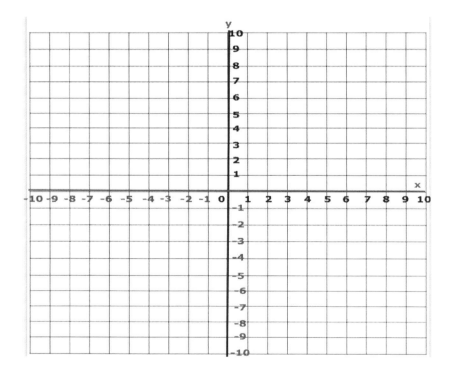

Unit 6 Lesson 11: Writing Quadratic Equations Given a Graph

MA.912.AR.1.2: Rearrange equations or formulas to isolate a quantity of interest.

MA.912.AR.3.8: Solve and graph mathematical and real-world problems that are modeled with quadratic functions. Interpret key features and determine constraints in terms of the context.

MA.912.AR.3.4: Write a quadratic function to represent the relationship between two quantities from a graph, a written description or a table of values within a mathematical or real-world context.

MA.912.AR.9.6: Given a real-world context, represent constraints as systems of linear equations or inequalities. Interpret solutions to problems as viable or non-viable options.

 # SHOW US WHAT YOU KNOW!

1) Graph the system of Equations and Write the solution to the system.

$2x - y = 7 \text{ and } x + 2y = -4$

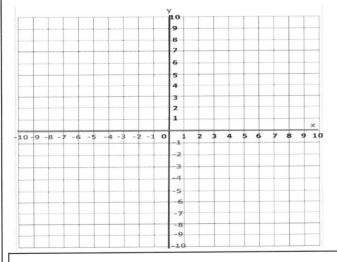

Solution: (,   )

BRAIN WORKOUT!
STEPS OF A LINE:

PARALLEL:

PERPENDICULAR:

DOMAIN:

RANGE:

X-INTERCEPT:

Y-INTERCEPT:

STEPS TO WRITING A QUADRATIC FUNCTION FROM A GRAPH GIVEN THE VERTEX

GOAL: Write a quadratic equation given a graph with a key feature.

1.	Locate the **vertex (h, k)** on the graph.
2.	Plug in the **vertex (h, k)** into the h and k in the Vertex Form equation. $$y = a(x - h)^2 + k$$
3.	Locate another **viable point** on the parabola **(x, y)** Plug in the point in the Vertex Form equation. $$y = a(x - h)^2 + k$$
4.	Solve for **a** using the Order of Operations, the Addition/Subtraction Property of Equality, and the Division Property of Equality
5.	Plug in the **a**, and the **vertex (h, k)** back into vertex form $$y = a(x - h)^2 + k$$

STEPS TO WRITING A QUADRATIC FUNCTION FROM A GRAPH GIVEN THE ZEROS, ROOTS, SOLUTIONS, X-INTERCEPT(S), GROUND

GOAL: Write a quadratic equation given a graph with a key feature.

3.	Locate the **roots, p and q,** on the graph.
4.	Plug in the **roots, p and q,** into the p and q in the Factored Form equation. $$y = a(x - p)(x - q)$$
3.	Locate another **viable point** on the parabola **(x, y)** Plug in the point in the Factored Form equation. $$y = a(x - p)(x - q)$$
4.	Solve for **a** using the Order of Operations, the Addition/Subtraction Property of Equality, and the Division Property of Equality
5.	Plug in the **a**, and the **roots, p and q,** back into factored form $$y = a(x - p)(x - q)$$

Write the equation for the Quadratic Function in vertex form, and standard form. Write the key features of the graph.

1) A football was thrown at an upward velocity of 32 feet per second.

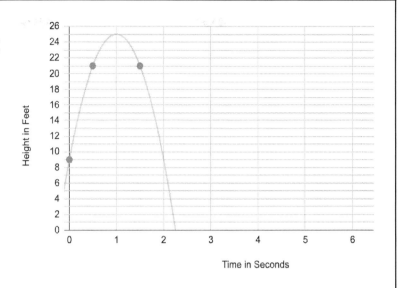

Vertex:	Interpret Vertex:	Viable Solution:
Vertex Form:		Standard Form:
Approximate x-intercept:		y-intercept:
Domain:		Range:
Increasing Interval:		Decreasing Interval:

2) A diver dove into the ocean. The graph models the divers path.

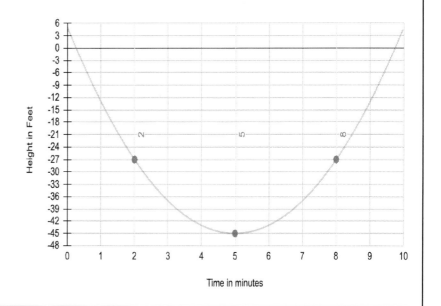

Height in Feet

Time in minutes

Vertex:	Interpret Vertex:	Viable Solution:
Vertex Form:		Standard Form:
Approximate x-intercept:		y-intercept:
Domain:		Range:
Increasing Interval:		Decreasing Interval:

3) A Rocket was launched at an upward Velocity of 20 Feet per second.

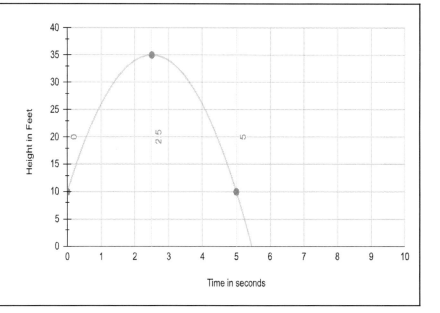

Height in Feet

Time in seconds

Vertex:	Interpret Vertex:	Viable Solution:
Vertex Form:		Standard Form:
Approximate x-intercept:		y-intercept:
Domain:		Range:
Increasing Interval:		Decreasing Interval:

1) Select all of the true statements about the graph given.

☐   (-8,0) is a viable solution

☐   (0,-8) is a viable solution

☐   Roots=-4 and 1

☐ $y = x^2 + 6x + 8$ is the standard form of the function.

☐ $y = 2x^2 + 6x - 8$ is the standard form of the function

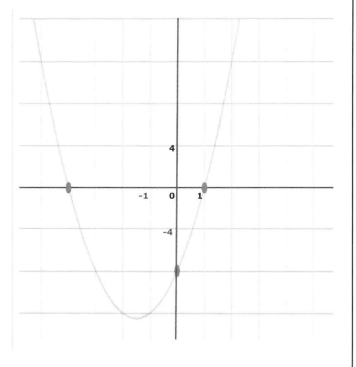

Unit 6 Lesson 12: Writing Quadratic Equations Given a Table

MA.912.AR.1.2: Rearrange equations or formulas to isolate a quantity of interest.

MA.912.AR.3.8: Solve and graph mathematical and real-world problems that are modeled with quadratic functions. Interpret key features and determine constraints in terms of the context.

MA.912.AR.3.4: Write a quadratic function to represent the relationship between two quantities from a graph, a written description or a table of values within a mathematical or real-world context.

MA.912.AR.9.6: Given a real-world context, represent constraints as systems of linear equations or inequalities. Interpret solutions to problems as viable or non-viable options.

 SHOW US WHAT YOU KNOW!

1)Lexie bought 4 packs of hotdogs and 2 packs of hamburgers for a total cost of $29.66. Yashi bought 3 packs of hotdogs and 5 packs of hamburgers for a total cost of $40.90. What was the cost of each hotdog?

Solution:

BRAIN WORKOUT!
Steps to:
Adding polynomials

Subtracting polynomials

Multiplying polynomials

Dividing polynomials

STEPS TO WRITING A QUADRATIC FUNCTION FROM A TABLE

GOAL: Write a quadratic equation given a table with a vertex.

1.	Locate the **vertex (h, k)** on the Table. * On the table look for where the y value repeats. The vertex is the point in between those 2 points.
2.	Plug in the **vertex (h, k)** into the h and k in the Vertex Form equation. $$y = a(x - h)^2 + k$$
3.	Locate another **viable point** on the parabola **(x, y)** Plug in the point in the Vertex Form equation. $$y = a(x - h)^2 + k$$
4.	Solve for **a** using the Order of Operations, the Addition/Subtraction Property of Equality, and the Division Property of Equality
5.	Plug in the **a**, and the **vertex (h, k)** back into vertex form $$y = a(x - h)^2 + k$$

Write the equation for the Quadratic Function in Vertex Form, and Standard Form. Write the key features of the graph.

1)

x	$f(x)$
-10	-396
-6	-204
4	-4
14	-204
16	-292

Vertex: $(4, -4)$	Viable Solution:
Vertex Form: $f(x) = -2(x-4)^2 - 4$	**Standard Form:** $f(x) = -2x^2 + 16x - 36$
y-intercept: -36	
Domain: all real numbers	Range: $y \leq -4$
Increasing Interval: $x < 4$	Decreasing Interval: $x > 4$

2)

t	$h(t)$
-1	20
0	0
1	-12
2	-16
3	-12

Vertex:	Viable Solution:
Vertex Form:	**Standard Form:**
y-intercept:	
Domain:	Range:
Increasing Interval:	Decreasing Interval:

3)

x	$g(x)$
-6	-24
-3	-6
0	0
3	-6
6	-24

Vertex:	Viable Solution:
Vertex Form:	**Standard Form:**
y-intercept:	
Domain:	Range:
Increasing Interval:	Decreasing Interval:

 TEST TIME!

1) Select all of the true statements about the Table given.

x	-5	0	5	12	13
y	-25	0	-25	-144	-169

☐ $a = 1$

☐ The parabola opens down.

☐ The parabola opens up.

☐ Vertex $= (5, -25)$

☐ Vertex $=$ the origin of the graph

☐ As x increases, y increases

☐ As x increases, y decreases

☐ As x decreases, y increases

☐ As x decreases, y decreases

Unit 6 Lesson 13: Write a Quadratic Function Given a Point and the X-intercepts

MA.912.AR.1.2: Rearrange equations or formulas to isolate a quantity of interest.

MA.912.AR.3.8: Solve and graph mathematical and real-world problems that are modeled with quadratic functions. Interpret key features and determine constraints in terms of the context.

MA.912.AR.3.5: Given the x-intercepts and another point on the graph of a quadratic function, write the equation for the function.

 SHOW US WHAT YOU KNOW!

1) A Quadratic Function is given. What is the Domain of the Function? What is the Range of the Function?

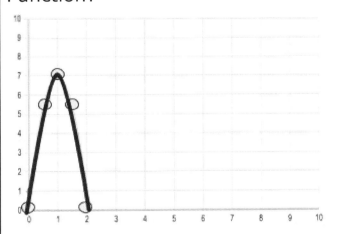

Domain:	Range:

BRAIN WORKOUT!
STEPS OF A QUADRATIC:

STEPS TO WRITING A QUADRATIC EQUATION GIVEN A POINT AND X-INTERCEPT(S)

GOAL: Write a Quadratic Function in Factored Form given the x-intercept(s) and a viable point.

1.	Replace the p and q with the x-intercept(s) of the function. $$y = a(x - p)(x - q)$$ *** If the function has only one solution, input the solution into both p and q!**
2.	Plug in the viable point (x, y) into the x and y in the equation. $$y = a(x - p)(x - q)$$ * **a** variable left in the equation, ALL other variables should be filled in with the numbers given.
3.	Solve for **a** using the Order of Operations and the Division Property of Equality.
4.	Solve for **a** using the Order of Operations, the Addition/Subtraction Property of Equality, and the Division Property of Equality
5.	Plug the **a** and the **x-intercept(s), p and q,** back into Factored Form. $$y = a(x - p)(x - q)$$

Write a Quadratic Function that passes through the point given and has the given x-intercepts. Write in Factored Form and Standard Form.

1)

$x-intercept$: $(2, 0), (-3, 0)$	*Passes through the point:* $(1, 8)$

Factored Form:

Standard Form:

Vertex Form:

2)

$x-intercept$: $(7, 0), (5, 0)$	*Passes through the point:* $(2, 15)$

Factored Form:

Standard Form:

Vertex Form:

3)

$x - intercept$: $(\frac{-2}{3}, 0), (-1, 0)$	Passes through the point: $(0, 10)$

Factored Form:

Standard Form:

Vertex Form:

4)

$x - intercept$: $(1, 0), (-1, 0)$	Passes through the point: $(2, 24)$

Factored Form:

Standard Form:

Vertex Form:

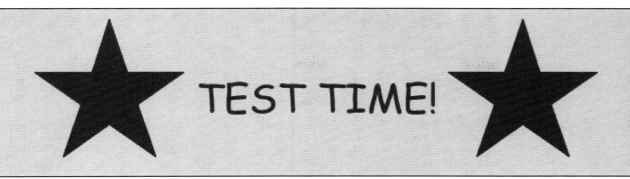

TEST TIME!

1) What is the vertex for the Quadratic Function that has the x-intercepts (-4,0) and (2,0) and passes through the point (0,-8).

Vertex:

Unit 6 Lesson 14: Quadratic Functions in Real World Context

MA.912.AR.1.2: Rearrange equations or formulas to isolate a quantity of interest.

MA.912.AR.3.7: Given a table, equation or written description of a quadratic function, graph that function, and determine and interpret its key features.

MA.912.AR.3.6: Given an expression or equation representing a quadratic function, determine the vertex and zeros and interpret them in terms of a real-world context.

MA.912.AR.9.6: Given a real-world context, represent constraints as systems of linear equations or inequalities. Interpret solutions to problems as viable or non-viable options.

MA.912.AR.3.8: Solve and graph mathematical and real-world problems that are modeled with quadratic functions. Interpret key features and determine constraints in terms of the context.

 SHOW US WHAT YOU KNOW!

1) Solve the inequality. Write 1 viable solution and 1 non-viable solution.

$3(x - 7) + 5 \geq 4x - 2 - x$

Viable	Non-Viable

BRAIN WORKOUT!
STEPS OF A LINE:

X-INTERCEPT:

Y-INTERCEPT:

VOCABULARY
QUADRATIC WORD PROBLEMS

THE Y (K) IN THE VERTEX	Maximum/minimum height Lowest/highest possible point
THE X IN THE VERTEX (H) AXIS OF SYMMETRY	Time to reach maximum/minimum $$x = \frac{-b}{2a}$$
ZEROS, ROOTS, GROUND, SOLUTIONS, X-INTERCEPT(S)	**Set the equation equal to zero and solve** **(x, 0)** Time it takes to reach the ground

Read each problem carefully, solve, and graph.

1) A football was thrown with an upward velocity of 60 feet per second. The height h, of the football after t seconds is given by the function

$$h = -15t^2 + 60t + 10.$$

a) How long will it take for the football to reach its maximum height?	
b) What is the football's maximum height?	
c) At what height was the ball released?	
d) At what time did the ball hit the ground?	
e) Write in Vertex Form:	

f) Domain:	g) Range:	h)

2) A golf ball was hit with an upward velocity of 108 feet per second. The height h, of the golf ball after t seconds is given by the function $h = 108t - 18t^2$.

a) How long will it take for the golf ball to reach its greatest height?	
b) What is the golf ball's greatest height?	
c) At what height was the golf ball initially, before it was hit?	
d) At what time did the ball hit the ground?	
e) Write in Vertex Form:	

f) Domain:	g) Range:	h)

3) A diver is jumping off a diving board with an initial upward velocity of 18 feet per second. The height h, of the diver after t seconds is given by the function $h = -(t - 9)^2 + 196$.

a) How long will it take for the diver to reach its maximum height?	
b) What is the divers maximum height?	
c) What was the initial height of the diving board?	
d) Write in Standard Form:	
e) Write in Factored Form:	
f) At what time will the diver enter the water?	

g) Domain:	h) Range:	i)

4) A volleyball was hit with an initial upward velocity of 14 feet per second. The height h, of the volleyball after t seconds is given by the function $h = -2(2t + 5)(t - 6)$.

a) How long will it take for the diver to reach its maximum height?	
b) What is the divers maximum height?	
c) What was the initial height of the diving board?	
d) Write in Vertex Form:	
e) Write in Standard Form:	
f) At what time did the volleyball hit the ground?	

g) Domain:	h) Range:	i)

TEST TIME!

1) A rocket was launched at an upward velocity of 64 feet per second. The height h, of the rocket after t seconds is given by the function $h = -16t^2 + 64t$. Graph the function. Label the Vertex and x-intercepts.

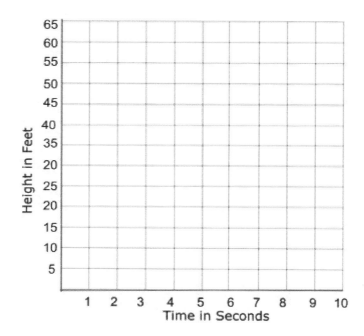

Unit 6 Lesson 15: Completing the Square

MA.912.AR.1.2: Rearrange equations or formulas to isolate a quantity of interest.

MA.912.AR.3.7: Given a table, equation or written description of a quadratic function, graph that function, and determine and interpret its key features.

MA.912.AR.3.6: Given an expression or equation representing a quadratic function, determine the vertex and zeros and interpret them in terms of a real-world context.

 SHOW US WHAT YOU KNOW!

1) Write an equivalent expression.

$$\left(\frac{2}{5}x - 7\right)\left(x - \frac{3}{2}\right)$$

BRAIN WORKOUT!
STEPS OF A LINE:

PARALLEL:

PERPENDICULAR:

STEPS TO COMPLETING THE SQUARE

GOAL: Write a quadratic equation given a table with a vertex.

1.	Label a, b , and c in quadratic standard form $$ax^2 + bx + c.$$ *If a=1 Skip steps 2-4.
2.	**If a>1:** Group a and b: $$(ax^2 + bx) + c.$$
3.	Factor a out and divide: $$a(\frac{a}{a}x^2 + \frac{b}{a}x) + c.$$
4.	Time to **COMPLETE THE SQUARE**: $$a(\frac{a}{a}x^2 + \frac{b}{a}x + \boxed{}) + c - a\boxed{}.$$
5.	Plug in a new c: $$\boxed{} = (\frac{b}{2})^2$$
6.	Combine: $$+ \ c - a\boxed{}$$
7.	The ( ) is now a perfect square trinomial!
8.	Rewrite as vertex form: $$a(x + \frac{b}{2})^2 + c - a\boxed{}$$

COMPLETE THE SQUARE.

1) $x^2 - 6x + 2$	**2)** $-x^2 - 4x - 4$

a:	b:	c:

a:	b:	c:

Vertex Form:

Axis of Symmetry:	
Vertex:	
$y-intercept$:	
Increasing Interval:	
Decreasing Interval:	
As $x \rightarrow \infty$	$y \rightarrow$
As $x \rightarrow -\infty$	$y \rightarrow$

Vertex Form:

Axis of Symmetry:	
Vertex:	
$y-intercept$:	
Increasing Interval:	
Decreasing Interval:	
As $x \rightarrow \infty$	$y \rightarrow$
As $x \rightarrow -\infty$	$y \rightarrow$

3) $2x^2 + 4x - 13$

a:	b:	c:

Vertex Form:

Axis of Symmetry:	
Vertex:	
$y - intercept$:	
Increasing Interval:	
Decreasing Interval:	
As $x \to \infty$	$y \to$
As $x \to -\infty$	$y \to$

4) $3x^2 - 24x + 7$

a:	b:	c:

Vertex Form:

Axis of Symmetry:	
Vertex:	
$y - intercept$:	
Increasing Interval:	
Decreasing Interval:	
As $x \to \infty$	$y \to$
As $x \to -\infty$	$y \to$

TEST TIME!

1) Ashlyn is completing the square for the Quadratic Function. In which step did she make her first error?

Given: $12x^2 - 48x + 7$

Step 1: $(12x^2 - 48x) + 7$

Step 2: $12(\frac{12x^2}{12} - \frac{48}{12}x) + 7$

Step 3: $12(x^2 - 4x + 4) + 7 - 4$

Step 4: $12(x - 2)^2 + 11$

Unit 6 Lesson 16: Solving Quadratic Equations Using Completing the Square

MA.912.AR.1.2: Rearrange equations or formulas to isolate a quantity of interest.

MA.912.AR.9.6: Given a real-world context, represent constraints as systems of linear equations or inequalities. Interpret solutions to problems as viable or non-viable options.

MA.912.AR.3.1: Given a mathematical or real-world context, write and solve one-variable quadratic equations over the real number system.

 SHOW US WHAT YOU KNOW!

1) Select all of the Viable Solutions to the Quadratic Function:

$$2x^2 + 4 = 36$$

☐ (4,0)

☐ (-4,0)

☐ (6,0)

☐ (0,6)

☐ (-6,0)

☐ (0,-6)

BRAIN WORKOUT!
STEPS OF A QUADRATIC:

STEPS TO SOLVING A QUADRATIC EQUATION BY COMPLETING THE SQUARE

GOAL: Solve for the zeros, roots, x-intercept(s) of the Quadratic Function. (BEST METHOD if a=1)	
1.	Set y=0, Use the Addition/Subtraction Property of Equality.
1.	Label a, b , and c in quadratic standard form $$ax^2 + bx + c = 0.$$ *If a=1 Skip steps 3-4.
2.	**If a>1:** Group a and b: $$(ax^2 + bx) + c = 0.$$
3.	Factor a out and divide: $$a(\frac{a}{a}x^2 + \frac{b}{a}x) + c = 0.$$
4.	Time to **COMPLETE THE SQUARE**: $$a(\frac{a}{a}x^2 + \frac{b}{a}x + \Box) + c - a\Box\ . = 0$$
5.	Plug in a new c: $$\Box = (\frac{b}{2})^2$$
6.	Combine: $$+\ c\ -a\Box$$
7.	The ( ) is now a perfect square trinomial! Rewrite as vertex form: $$a(x + \frac{b}{2})^2 + c - a\Box = 0$$
8.	Solve for X: Use the Addition/Subtraction Property of Equality, the Multiplication Property of Equality/Division Property of Equality, and then Square Root both sides of the equation.

Solve the Quadratic Function by completing the square. Write down the key features of the graph.

1) $x^2 - 6x + 2 = -11$

a:	b:	c:

Vertex Form:

$x - intercept(s)$:		

$Axis\ of\ Symmetry$:	
$Vertex$:	
$y - intercept$:	
$Increasing\ Interval$:	
$Decreasing\ Interval$:	
$As\ x \to \infty$	$y \to$
$As\ x \to -\infty$	$y \to$

2) $x^2 + 4x - 4 = 8$

a:	b:	c:

Vertex Form:

$x - intercept(s)$:		

$Axis\ of\ Symmetry$:	
$Vertex$:	
$y - intercept$:	
$Increasing\ Interval$:	
$Decreasing\ Interval$:	
$As\ x \to \infty$	$y \to$
$As\ x \to -\infty$	$y \to$

3) $2x^2 + 4x - 13 = 113$

a:	b:	c:

Vertex Form:

$x - intercept(s)$:		

$Axis\ of\ Symmetry$:	
$Vertex$:	
$y - intercept$:	
$Increasing$ $Interval$:	
$Decreasing$ $Interval$:	
$As\ x \to \infty$	$y \to$
$As\ x \to -\infty$	$y \to$

4) $3x^2 - 24x + 7 = 7$

a:	b:	c:

Vertex Form:

$x - intercept(s)$:		

$Axis\ of\ Symmetry$:	
$Vertex$:	
$y - intercept$:	
$Increasing$ $Interval$:	
$Decreasing$ $Interval$:	
$As\ x \to \infty$	$y \to$
$As\ x \to -\infty$	$y \to$

 **TEST TIME!**

1) Select all of the solutions to the Quadratic Function:

$$x^2 - 4x + 3 = -4$$

☐ $(4, 0)$

☐ $(0, 0)$

☐ *The roots to the equation is no real solution*

☐ $x - intercept\ is\ no\ real\ solution$

☐ *The zeros of the Function is no real solution*

Unit 7 - Absolute Value Functions

Unit 7 Lesson 1: Solving and Writing Absolute Value Equations

MA.912.AR.4.1: Given a mathematical or real-world context, write and solve one-variable absolute value equations.

 SHOW US WHAT YOU KNOW!

1) Write the function in vertex form.

$$y = -x^2 - 26x + 10$$

Vertex Form:

BRAIN WORKOUT!
STEPS OF AN EXPONENTIAL

VOCABULARY

Function	For every input there is exactly one output. The x values cannot repeat!
Linear Function	A function that creates a straight line. Degree = Largest exponent on variable = 1 **1) Slope = Constant Rate of Change =** $$m = \frac{y_2 - y_1}{x_2 - x_1}$$ **2) Point-Slope Form:** $y - y_1 = m(x - x_1)$ **3) Slope-Intercept Form:** $y = mx + b$ **4) Standard Form:** $Ax + By = C$
Quadratic Function	A function that creates a parabola. Degree = Largest exponent on variable = 2 **1) Standard Form:** $$y = ax^2 + bx \boxed{+ c}$$ Y-intercept Initial value

To Find Vertex:	
Axis of symmetry: $x = h = \frac{-b}{2a}$	**Plug in x to get y=k** **This is your range**

2) Quadratic Formula:
$$x = \frac{-b \pm \sqrt{b^2 - 4ac}}{2a} = p \text{ and } q$$

3) Vertex Form: $y = a(x - h)^2 + k$
    (h, k) = Vertex

4) Factored Form: $y = a(x - p)(x - q)$
    p and q represent x-intercepts

To Find Vertex:	
Axis of symmetry: $x = h = \frac{p+q}{2}$	**Plug in x to get y=k** **This is your range**

# Absolute Value	1) Vertex Form: $$y = \boxed{a}|x - h| + k$$ **Slope** a = + (Opens up) a = - (Opens down) **Vertex = (h, k)** h = Axis of Symmetry k = range 2) X-intercepts 1) Plug 0 into y 2) Isolate the Absolute value on one side | One Solution: $\| \| = 0$	Two Solutions: $\| \| = +$	No Solution: $\| \| = -$	

# X-INTERCEPT	(x,0) Plug in 0 into y
# Y-INTERCEPT	(0,y) Plug in 0 into X
# DOMAIN # X	Set of inputs in the function. The independent variable. Time
# RANGE # Y=f(x)	Set of outputs in the function. The dependent variable. Total once you input x value.
# VIABLE	The inputs and outputs satisfy the functions constraints.
# NON -VIABLE	The inputs and outputs DO NOT satisfy the functions constraints.

STEPS TO SOLVING ABSOLUTE VALUE EQUATIONS

GOAL: Solve for the zeros, roots, x-intercept(s), solutions of the Absolute Value ||
1.	Isolate the Absolute value symbol, cancel all numbers on the outside of the | |.
2.	Once all numbers are canceled on the outside of the absolute value symbol, determine the number of solutions.

$\| \| = -$	$\| \| = +$	$\| \| = 0$
NO SOLUTION	**TWO SOLUTIONS**	**ONE SOLUTION**

3.	**NOW IT'S TIME TO SOLVE!**

$\| \| = -$	$\| \| = +$	$\| \| = 0$
Write NO SOLUTION	**TWO SOLUTIONS**	**ONE SOLUTION**
	1. Take out the absolute value symbol and solve for the variable using properties 2. Rewrite the equation, but this time make the total **NEGATIVE** and solve!	1. Take out the absolute value symbol and solve for the variable using properties

Solve for the given variable.

1) $3 = \lvert x \rvert$	2) $\lvert x \rvert = -3$
3) $2\lvert -2x - 7 \rvert + 4 = 4$	4) $13 = -\lvert -4x + 8 \rvert - 7$
5) $6\lvert x \rvert + 12 = 24$	6) $-\lvert x - 7 \rvert - 25 = 26$
7) $-9\lvert x - 3 \rvert + 81 = 0$	8) $\lvert x + 23 \rvert - 16 = 0$
9) $\lvert x \rvert = 0$	10) $\lvert x \rvert + 17 = 8$

Write and solve the absolute value equation given the real world context.

11) Ben gets an average of 6 touchdowns in a season but can range by 2 touchdowns. What is the maximum and minimum touchdowns in a season for Ben?

Equation:

Maximum:	Minimum:

12) The average temperature is 63° in January with a difference of 5°. What is the maximum and minimum temperature for January?

Equation:

Maximum:	Minimum

13) Anderson averages 95% on his math exams. He has a margin of error of about 4%. What are the maximum and minimum test grades Anderson has earned?

Equation:

Maximum:	Minimum:

14) Santiago gets an average of $300 for tutoring each week. This varies about $20, depending on the number of jobs he gets a week. What is the maximum and minimum amount Santiago makes in a week?

Equation:

Maximum:	Minimum:

TEST TIME!

1) Select all of the solutions to the equation:

$$-8|3x - 7| + 4 = -12$$

☐ No Solution

☐ $x = 3$

☐ $x = -3$

☐ $x = \dfrac{5}{3}$

☐ $x = \dfrac{-5}{3}$

☐ Infinite Solutions

Unit 7 Lesson 2: Key Features of Absolute Value Equations

MA.912.AR.4.1: Given a mathematical or real-world context, write and solve one-variable absolute value equations.

MA.912.AR.4.3: Given a table, equation or written description of an absolute value function, graph that function and determine its key features.

  SHOW US WHAT YOU KNOW!

1) An Electrician charges a $30 flat fee and $85 per hour. Write an equation to model this situation. Use h for hours and C(h) for the total charge.

BRAIN WORKOUT!
STEPS FOR A QUADRATIC:

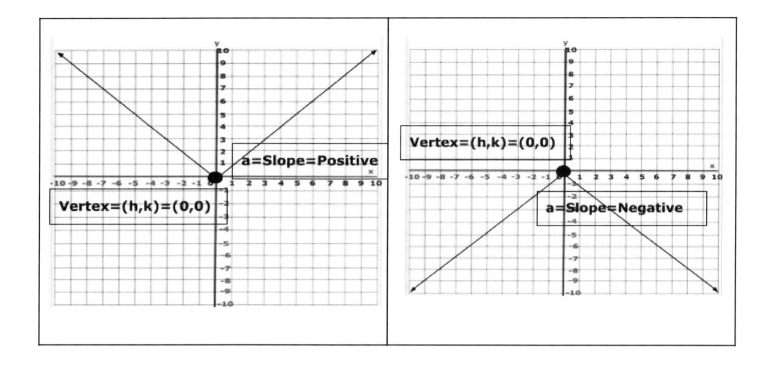

Vertex=(h,k)=(0,0)
a=Slope=Positive

Vertex=(h,k)=(0,0)
a=Slope=Negative

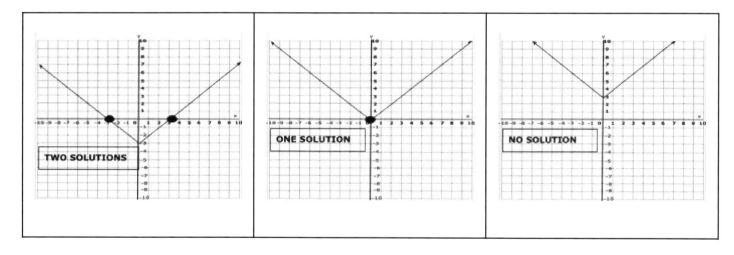

TWO SOLUTIONS

ONE SOLUTION

NO SOLUTION

Vertex Form: $y = a\|x - h\| + k$	
Example: $y = \frac{1}{2}\|x + 4\| - 3$ 1) Label a, h, k a=$\frac{1}{2}$ h=-4 k=-3	2) Axis of Symmetry=h=x in vertex h=x=-4
3) Maximum=k=a must be negative Minimum=k=a must be positive Minimum=-3	4)Vertex=(h,k): (-4,-3)
5)Solutions=x-intercept=(x,0) Plug in 0 into y to solve for x. $0 = \frac{1}{2}\|x + 4\| - 3$ $0 + 3 = \frac{1}{2}\|x + 4\| - 3 + 3$ $3 = \frac{1}{2}\|x + 4\|$ $3 \bullet 2 = \frac{1}{2} \bullet 2\|x + 4\|$ $6 = \|x + 4\|$ $x + 4 = 6 \; or \; x + 4 =- 6$ $x + 4 - 4 = 6 - 4 \; or \; x + 4 - 4 =- 6 - 4$ $x = 2 \; or \; x =- 10$ Two Solutions	6) Domain= x values: $- \infty \leq x \leq \infty$
7) Range= y values:	8) Increasing/Decreasing Interval

a=+	a=-
$y \geq k$	$y \leq k$

$y \geq \; - 3$

a=+	a=-
Increasing: $x > h$	*Increasing*: $x < h$
decreasing: $x < h$	*decreasing*: $x > h$
As $x \to \infty, \; y \to \infty$	*As* $x \to \infty, \; y \to - \infty$
As $x \to - \infty, \; y \to \infty$	*As* $x \to - \infty, \; y \to - \infty$

Increasing: x>-4
Decreasing: x<-4
As $x \to \infty, \; y \to \infty$
As $x \to - \infty, \; y \to \infty$

Write down the key features of the Equation given.

1) $y = |x|$

a:	h:	k:

Maximum or Minimum:	
Axis of Symmetry:	
Vertex:	
Solutions:	☐ One ☐ Two ☐ None
Domain:	
Range:	
Increasing Interval:	
Decreasing Interval:	
As $x \to \infty$	$y \to$
As $x \to -\infty$	$y \to$
Viable Solution:	Non − Viable Solution:

2) $y = -|x|$

a:	h:	k:

Maximum or Minimum:	
Axis of Symmetry:	
Vertex:	
Solutions:	☐ One ☐ Two ☐ None
Domain:	
Range:	
Increasing Interval:	
Decreasing Interval:	
As $x \to \infty$	$y \to$
As $x \to -\infty$	$y \to$
Viable Solution:	Non − Viable Solution:

3) $y = -\frac{4}{5}|x - 7| + 4$

a:	h:	k:

Maximum or Minimum:	
Axis of Symmetry:	
Vertex:	
Solutions:	☐ One ☐ Two ☐ None
Domain:	
Range:	
Increasing Interval:	
Decreasing Interval:	
As $x \to \infty$	$y \to$
As $x \to -\infty$	$y \to$
Viable Solution:	Non − Viable Solution:

4) $y = \frac{1}{2}|x + 8|$

a:	h:	k:

Maximum or Minimum:	
Axis of Symmetry:	
Vertex:	
Solutions:	☐ One ☐ Two ☐ None
Domain:	
Range:	
Increasing Interval:	
Decreasing Interval:	
As $x \to \infty$	$y \to$
As $x \to -\infty$	$y \to$
Viable Solution:	Non − Viable Solution:

5) $y = -|x - 2| - 5$

a:	h:	k:

Maximum or Minimum:	
Axis of Symmetry:	
Vertex:	
Solutions:	☐ One ☐ Two ☐ None
Domain:	
Range:	
Increasing Interval:	
Decreasing Interval:	
As $x \to \infty$	$y \to$
As $x \to -\infty$	$y \to$
Viable Solution:	Non − Viable Solution:

6) $y = |x| + 7$

a:	h:	k:

Maximum or Minimum:	
Axis of Symmetry:	
Vertex:	
Solutions:	☐ One ☐ Two ☐ None
Domain:	
Range:	
Increasing Interval:	
Decreasing Interval:	
As $x \to \infty$	$y \to$
As $x \to -\infty$	$y \to$
Viable Solution:	Non − Viable Solution:

TEST TIME!

1) Select all of the true statements about the graph

☐ The graph Represents an Absolute Value Function

☐ The graph Represents a Linear Function

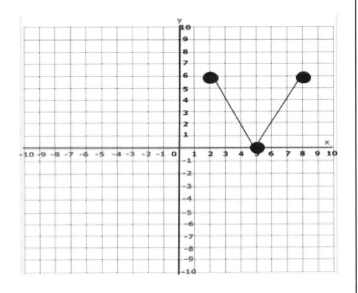

☐ Vertex=(0,5)

☐ Vertex=(5,0)

☐ Axis of symmetry:x=5

☐ a is positive

☐ a is negative

☐ Domain: $2 \leq x \leq 8$

☐ Range:$2 \leq y \leq 8$

☐ Range: $0 \leq y \leq 6$

Unit 7 Lesson 3: Graphing Key Features of Absolute Value Functions

MA.912.AR.4.1: Given a mathematical or real-world context, write and solve one-variable absolute value equations.

MA.912.AR.4.3: Given a table, equation or written description of an absolute value function, graph that function and determine its key features.

 SHOW US WHAT YOU KNOW!

1) What is the Domain and Range of the Function?

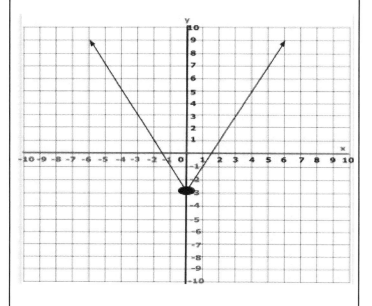

Domain:	Range:

BRAIN WORKOUT!
STEPS OF A LINE:

PARALLEL:

PERPENDICULAR:

DOMAIN:

RANGE:

X-INTERCEPT:

Y-INTERCEPT:

Graph the Function. Write down the key features.

1) EXAMPLE: $y = |x|$

a: 1	h: 0	k: 0

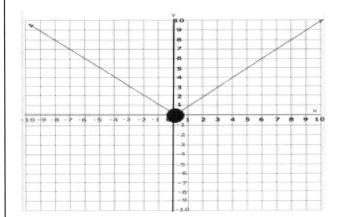

Maximum/Minimum:	Minimum=0
Axis of Symmetry:	x=0
Vertex:	(0,0)
y − intercept:	(0,0)
x − intercept(s):	(0,0)
Domain:	$-\infty \leq x \leq \infty$
Range:	$y \geq 0$
Increasing Interval:	$x > 0$
Decreasing Interval:	$x < 0$
As $x \rightarrow \infty$	$y \rightarrow \infty$
As $x \rightarrow -\infty$	$y \rightarrow \infty$
Viable Solution: (1,1)	Non − Viable: (-3,-3)

2) $y = -|x| + 5$

a:	h:	k:

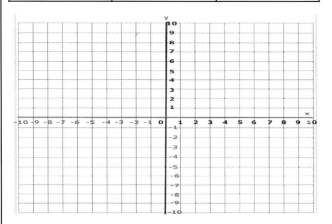

Maximum/Minimum:	
Axis of Symmetry:	
Vertex:	
y − intercept:	
x − intercept(s):	
Domain:	
Range:	
Increasing Interval:	
Decreasing Interval:	
As $x \rightarrow \infty$	$y \rightarrow$
As $x \rightarrow -\infty$	$y \rightarrow$
Viable Solution:	Non − Viable:

3) $y = -\frac{2}{3}|x - 6| + 3$		
a:	h:	k:

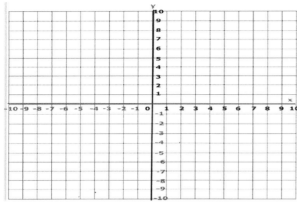

Maximum/Minimum:	
Axis of Symmetry:	
Vertex:	
$y - intercept$:	
$x - intercept(s)$:	
Domain:	
Range:	
Increasing Interval:	
Decreasing Interval:	
As $x \to \infty$	$y \to$
As $x \to -\infty$	$y \to$
Viable Solution:	Non − Viable:

4) $y = \frac{1}{5}|x + 7|$		
a:	h:	k:

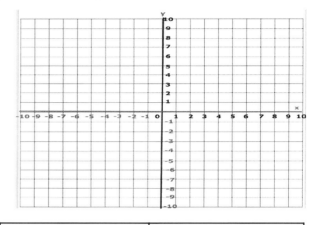

Maximum/Minimum:	
Axis of Symmetry:	
Vertex:	
$y - intercept$:	
$x - intercept(s)$:	
Domain:	
Range:	
Increasing Interval:	
Decreasing Interval:	
As $x \to \infty$	$y \to$
As $x \to -\infty$	$y \to$
Viable Solution:	Non − Viable:

5) $y = -|x - 1| - 9$		
a:	h:	k:

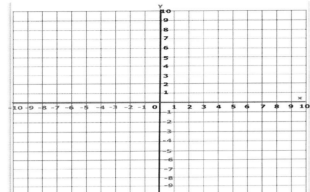

Maximum/Minimum:	
Axis of Symmetry:	
Vertex:	
$y - intercept$:	
$x - intercept(s)$:	
Domain:	
Range:	
Increasing Interval:	
Decreasing Interval:	
As $x \to \infty$	$y \to$
As $x \to -\infty$	$y \to$
Viable Solution:	Non − Viable:

6) $y = |x + 8| + 3$		
a:	h:	k:

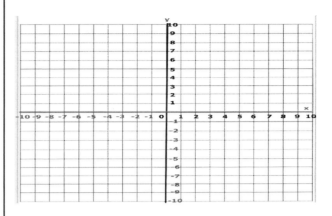

Maximum/Minimum:	
Axis of Symmetry:	
Vertex:	
$y - intercept$:	
$x - intercept(s)$:	
Domain:	
Range:	
Increasing Interval:	
Decreasing Interval:	
As $x \to \infty$	$y \to$
As $x \to -\infty$	$y \to$
Viable Solution:	Non − Viable:

TEST TIME!

1) Select all of the true statements about the graph

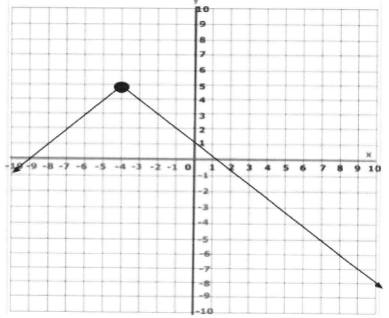

☐ The graph represents an Absolute Value Function

☐ The graph represents a Quadratic Function

☐ Vertex=(-4,5)

☐ Vertex=(5,-4)

☐ Axis of symmetry:x=-4

☐ a is positive

☐ a is negative

☐ Domain: $-9 \leq x \leq 1$

☐ Domain:$-\infty \leq x \leq \infty$

☐ Range: $-\infty \leq y \leq 5$

☐ Range: $0 \leq y \leq 6$

Unit 7 Lesson 4: Graphing Key Features of Absolute Value Functions given a table

MA.912.AR.4.1: Given a mathematical or real-world context, write and solve one-variable absolute value equations.

MA.912.AR.4.3: Given a table, equation or written description of an absolute value function, graph that function and determine its key features.

 SHOW US WHAT YOU KNOW!

1) Write the equation for the function? What is the Domain and Range of the Function?

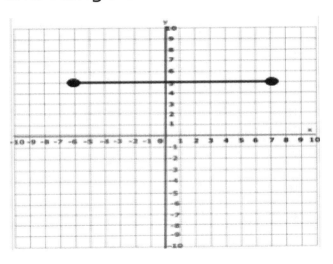

Equation:

Domain:	Range:

BRAIN WORKOUT!
STEPS OF A ABSOLUTE VALUE:

Find the vertex and the a for each table. Write the equation for the function, graph the function and write down the key features.

1)

x	2	3	4	5
$f(x)$	6	4	6	8

Equation:

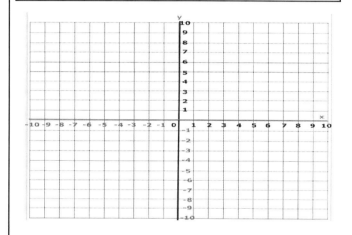

Maximum/Minimum:	
Axis of Symmetry:	
Vertex:	
Domain:	
Range:	
As x $\to \infty$	$y \to$
As x $\to -\infty$	$y \to$
x – intercept:	*y – intercept*:

2)

x	-6	-3	0	3
y	6	8	6	4

Equation:

Maximum/Minimum:	
Axis of Symmetry:	
Vertex:	
Domain:	
Range:	
As x $\to \infty$	$y \to$
As x $\to -\infty$	$y \to$
x – intercept:	*y – intercept*:

Fill in the table for the given function. Graph the Function. Write the Key Features of the Function.

3) $f(x) = |x + 5| - 1$

x	$f(x) = |x + 5| - 1$	$f(x)$

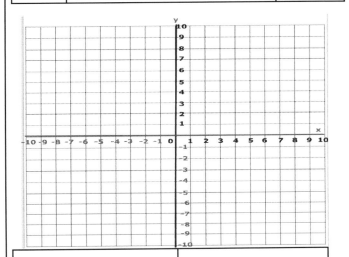

Maximum/Minimum:	
Axis of Symmetry:	
Vertex:	
Domain:	
Range:	
As $x \to \infty$	$y \to$
As $x \to -\infty$	$y \to$
$x - intercept$:	$y - intercept$:

4) $y = -\frac{1}{2}|x - 8|$

x	$y = -\frac{1}{2}|x - 8|$	y

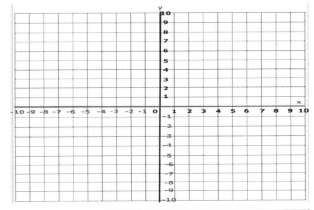

Maximum/Minimum:	
Axis of Symmetry:	
Vertex:	
Domain:	
Range:	
As $x \to \infty$	$y \to$
As $x \to -\infty$	$y \to$
$x - intercept$:	$y - intercept$:

1) The table represents an absolute value function. Write an equation for the function and complete the missing points.

x	h(x)
-5	-5
-4	-2
-3	-5
0	
	-20

Unit 8 - Exponential Functions

Unit 8 Lesson 1: Key Features of Exponential Equations

MA.912.AR.5.3: Given a mathematical or real-world context, classify an exponential function as representing growth or decay.

MA.912.AR.5.6: Given a table, equation or written description of an exponential function, graph that function and determine its key features.

 SHOW US WHAT YOU KNOW!

1) Write the equation for the function in vertex form.

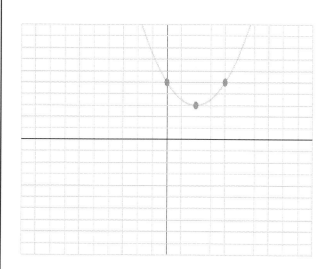

Vertex Form:

BRAIN WORKOUT!
STEPS OF A LINE:

PARALLEL:

PERPENDICULAR:

DOMAIN:

RANGE:

X-INTERCEPT:

Y-INTERCEPT:

VOCABULARY

Function	For every input there is exactly one output. The x values cannot repeat!
Linear Function	A function that creates a straight line. Degree = Largest exponent on variable = 1 **1) Slope = Constant Rate of Change =** $$m = \frac{y_2 - y_1}{x_2 - x_1}$$ **2) Point-Slope Form:** $y - y_1 = m(x - x_1)$ **3) Slope-Intercept Form:** $y = mx + b$ **4) Standard Form:** $Ax + By = C$
Quadratic Function	A function that creates a parabola. Degree = Largest exponent on variable = 2 **1) Standard Form:** $$y = ax^2 + bx \boxed{+ c} \quad \text{Y-intercept Initial value}$$

To Find Vertex:	
Axis of symmetry: $x = h = \frac{-b}{2a}$	**Plug in x to get y=k** **This is your range**

2) Quadratic Formula:
$$x = \frac{-b \pm \sqrt{b^2 - 4ac}}{2a} = p \text{ and } q$$
3) Vertex Form: $y = a(x - h)^2 + k$
    (h, k) = Vertex
4) Factored Form: $y = a(x - p)(x - q)$
    p and q represent x-intercepts

To Find Vertex:	
Axis of symmetry: $x = h = \frac{p+q}{2}$	**Plug in x to get y=k** **This is your range**

Absolute Value

1) **Vertex Form:**

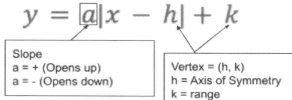

$$y = \boxed{a}|x - h| + k$$

Slope
a = + (Opens up)
a = - (Opens down)

Vertex = (h, k)
h = Axis of Symmetry
k = range

2) X-intercepts

> 3) Plug 0 into y
> 4) Isolate the Absolute value on one side

One Solution:	Two Solutions:	No Solution:
| | = 0	| | = +	| | = −

Exponential Function

1) **Standard Form:**

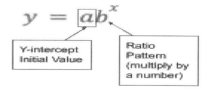

$$y = \boxed{a}\boxed{b}^{x}$$

Y-intercept Initial Value

Ratio Pattern (multiply by a number)

2) **Exponential Growth with %:**

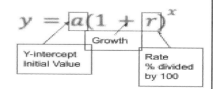

$$y = \boxed{a}(1 + \boxed{r})^{x}$$

Growth

Y-intercept Initial Value

Rate % divided by 100

3) **Exponential Decay with %:**

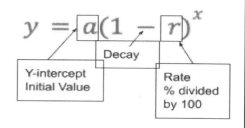

$$y = \boxed{a}(1 - \boxed{r})^{x}$$

Decay

Y-intercept Initial Value

Rate % divided by 100

X-INTERCEPT	(x,0) Plug in 0 into y
Y-INTERCEPT	(0,y) Plug in 0 into X
DOMAIN X	Set of inputs in the function. The independent variable. Time
RANGE Y=f(x)	Set of outputs in the function. The dependent variable. Total once you input x value.
VIABLE	The inputs and outputs satisfy the functions constraints.
NON -VIABLE	The inputs and outputs DO NOT satisfy the functions constraints.

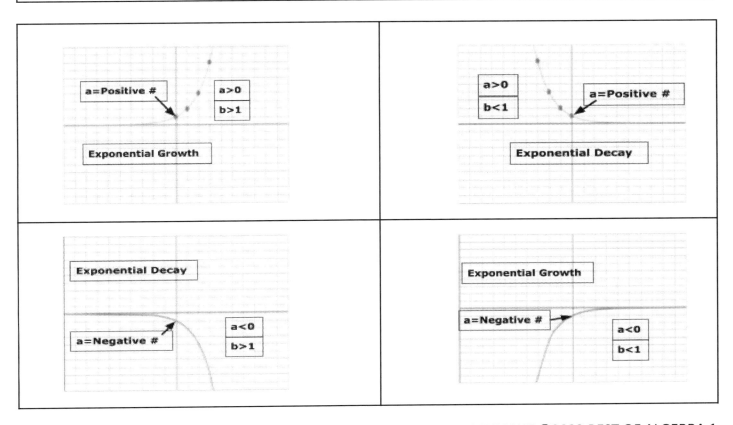

Write down the key features of the Equation given.

1) Example: $y = 2^x$

a: 1	b: 2

b>1 Growth
0<b<1 Decay

a=positive, range: y>
a=negative, range: y<

$y = 2^x$
$y = 2^1$
$y = 2$

Exponential:	☑ Growth ☐ Decay
Ratio:	Times 2
Asymptote:	k=0
$y - intercept$:	(0,1)
Domain:	$-\infty \le x \le \infty$
Range:	$y > 0$
As $x \to \infty$	$y \to \infty$
As $x \to -\infty$	$y \to 0$
Viable Solution: (1,2)	Non − Viable: (-1,-2)

2) $y = -2^x$

a:	b:

Exponential:	☐ Growth ☐ Decay
Ratio:	
Asymptote:	
$y - intercept$:	
Domain:	
Range:	
As $x \to \infty$	$y \to$
As $x \to -\infty$	$y \to$
Viable Solution:	Non − Viable:

3) $y = -4\left(\frac{1}{2}\right)^x$

a:	b:

Exponential:	☐ Growth ☐ Decay
Ratio:	
Asymptote:	
$y-intercept$:	
Domain:	
Range:	
As $x \to \infty$	$y \to$
As $x \to -\infty$	$y \to$
Viable Solution:	Non − Viable:

4) $y = 7(3)^x$

a:	b:

Exponential:	☐ Growth ☐ Decay
Ratio:	
Asymptote:	
$y-intercept$:	
Domain:	
Range:	
As $x \to \infty$	$y \to$
As $x \to -\infty$	$y \to$
Viable Solution:	Non − Viable:

5) $y = -(0.3)^x$

a:	b:

Exponential:	☐ Growth ☐ Decay
Ratio:	
Asymptote:	
$y-intercept$:	
Domain:	
Range:	
As $x \to \infty$	$y \to$
As $x \to -\infty$	$y \to$
Viable Solution:	Non − Viable:

6) $y = 12\left(\frac{2}{5}\right)^x$

a:	b:

Exponential:	☐ Growth ☐ Decay
Ratio:	
Asymptote:	
$y-intercept$:	
Domain:	
Range:	
As $x \to \infty$	$y \to$
As $x \to -\infty$	$y \to$
Viable Solution:	Non − Viable:

TEST TIME!

1) Select all of the key features of the Exponential function.

$$f(x) = -10(4)^x$$

☐ $(0, -10)$ $is\ the\ y-intercept$

☐ $(0, 4)$ $is\ the\ y-intercept$

☐ $-10\ is\ the\ common\ ratio$

☐ $4\ is\ the\ common\ ratio$

☐ $This\ Function\ represents\ an\ Exponential\ Growth.$

☐ $This\ Function\ represents\ an\ Exponential\ Decay.$

☐ $b < 1$

☐ $b > 1$

Unit 8 Lesson 2: Graphing Key Features of Exponential Equations

MA.912.AR.5.3: Given a mathematical or real-world context, classify an exponential function as representing growth or decay.

MA.912.AR.5.6: Given a table, equation or written description of an exponential function, graph that function and determine its key features.

 SHOW US WHAT YOU KNOW!

1) Select all of the true statements about the function $y = -|x| + 5$

☐ It represents an Absolute value function.

☐ It represents a quadratic function.

☐ It represents an Exponential function.

☐ a = -1

☐ a = 1

☐ The Vertex = (0, 5)

☐ The Vertex = (1, 5)

☐ The equation has One solution.

☐ The equation has Two solutions.

☐ The equation has No solution.

BRAIN WORKOUT!
WRITE THE INEQUALITIES SYMBOLS AND NAME THEM:

STEPS TO GRAPHING AN EXPONENTIAL FUNCTION

GOAL: Graph exponential functions using key features.

1.	Plot the **a = y-intercept = (0,y)**
2.	Plug in **1** into the **x** in the equation $y = ab^x$ and solve for **y**.
3.	Plot the **point (x, y)**.
4.	If b>1: Exponential Growth
5.	If b<1: Exponential Decay

Find the key features of the equation, then graph the equation.

1) $y = 7^x$

a:	b:
Viable Solution:	

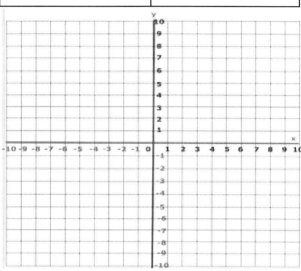

Exponential:	☐ Growth ☐ Decay
$x - intercepts$:	
$y - intercept$:	
Domain:	
Range:	
As $x \to \infty$	$y \to$
As $x \to -\infty$	$y \to$

2) $y = -7^x$

a:	b:
Viable Solution:	

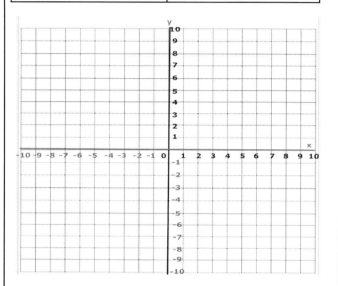

Exponential:	☐ Growth ☐ Decay
$x - intercepts$:	
$y - intercept$:	
Domain:	
Range:	
As $x \to \infty$	$y \to$
As $x \to -\infty$	$y \to$

3) $y = 2(\frac{1}{2})^x$

a:	b:
Viable Solution:	

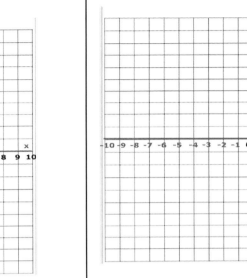

Exponential:	☐ Growth ☐ Decay
$x-intercepts$:	
$y-intercept$:	
Domain:	
Range:	
As $x \to \infty$	$y \to$
As $x \to -\infty$	$y \to$

4) $y = -3(\frac{2}{3})^x$

a:	b:
Viable Solution:	

Exponential:	☐ Growth ☐ Decay
$x-intercepts$:	
$y-intercept$:	
Domain:	
Range:	
As $x \to \infty$	$y \to$
As $x \to -\infty$	$y \to$

TEST TIME!

1) Graph the Function

$$y = -4\left(\frac{1}{2}\right)^{x}$$

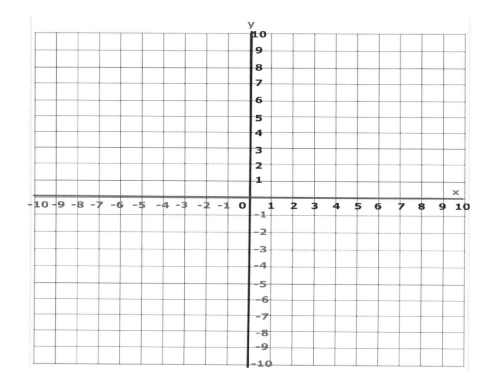

Unit 8 Lesson 3: Graphing Key Features of Exponential Equations Given a Table

MA.912.AR.5.3: Given a mathematical or real-world context, classify an exponential function as representing growth or decay.

MA.912.AR.5.6: Given a table, equation or written description of an exponential function, graph that function and determine its key features.

 SHOW US WHAT YOU KNOW!

1) Classify each function as Linear, Quadratic, Absolute Value or Exponential.

a) $2x^2 - 5 = y + 3$

b) $y - 3 = |x| + 4$

c) $y + 3 = \frac{1}{2}(x - 7)$

d) $2^x - 5 = y$

BRAIN WORKOUT!
STEPS OF A LINE:

PARALLEL:

PERPENDICULAR:

DOMAIN:

RANGE:

X-INTERCEPT:

Y-INTERCEPT:

Find a and b. Write the equation for the function, graph the function, then write down the key features.

1)

x	1	2	3	4
$f(x)$	2	4	8	16

a:	b:

Equation:

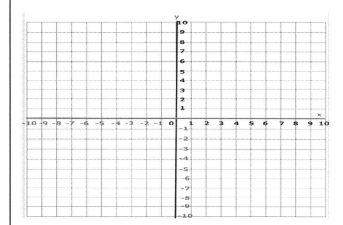

Exponential:	☐ Growth ☐ Decay
$x-intercept(s)$:	
$y-intercept$:	
Domain:	
Range:	
As $x \to \infty$	$y \to$
As $x \to -\infty$	$y \to$

2)

x	-4	-3	-2	-1
y	128	64	32	16

a:	b:

Equation:

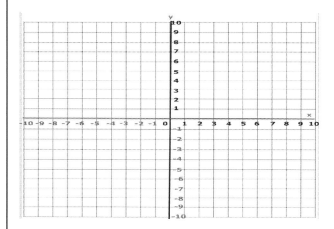

Exponential:	☐ Growth ☐ Decay
$x-intercept(s)$:	
$y-intercept$:	
Domain:	
Range:	
As $x \to \infty$	$y \to$
As $x \to -\infty$	$y \to$

3)

Equation: $f(x) = 2(\frac{1}{3})^x$	
a:	b:

x	$f(x) = 2(\frac{1}{3})^x$	$f(x)$

Exponential:	☐ Growth ☐ Decay
$x - intercept(s)$:	
$y - intercept$:	
Domain:	
Range:	
As $x \to \infty$	$y \to$
As $x \to -\infty$	$y \to$

4)

Equation: $f(x) = -2(\frac{3}{2})^x$	
a:	b:

x	$f(x) = -2(\frac{3}{2})^x$	$f(x)$

Exponential:	☐ Growth ☐ Decay
$x - intercept(s)$:	
$y - intercept$:	
Domain:	
Range:	
As $x \to \infty$	$y \to$
As $x \to -\infty$	$y \to$

TEST TIME!

1) The table represents a function. Write an equation for the function and complete the missing points.

x	f(x)
-1	64
0	16
1	4
	1
3	

Unit 8 Lesson 4: Writing Exponential Equations Given a Graph

MA.912.AR.5.3: Given a mathematical or real-world context, classify an exponential function as representing growth or decay.

MA.912.AR.5.4: Write an exponential function to represent a relationship between two quantities from a graph, a written description or a table of values within a mathematical or real-world context.

 SHOW US WHAT YOU KNOW!

1) Select all of the true statements about the function $2y - 6 = -7x$

☐ It represents a linear function.

☐ It represents a quadratic function.

☐ It represents an Exponential function.

☐ The rate of change is -7.

☐ The rate of change is $\frac{-7}{2}$.

☐ The initial value is -6.

☐ The initial value is 3.

☐ (2,-4) is a viable solution.

BRAIN WORKOUT!
STEPS OF A LINE:

PARALLEL:

PERPENDICULAR:

DOMAIN:

RANGE:

X-INTERCEPT:

Y-INTERCEPT:

STEPS TO WRITING AN EXPONENTIAL FUNCTION GIVEN A GRAPH

GOAL: Write an exponential function given a graph with key features.

1.	Plot the **a = y-intercept = (0,y)**
2.	Plug in a into $y = ab^x$
3.	Find a **viable solution** on the graph **(x, y)** *Do not use the y-intercept again! *Try to use (1, y)
4.	Plug in Point **(x, y)** and **a** into $y = ab^x$.
5.	Solve for **b**. Use the Division Property of Equality and the roots to cancel a and x.
6.	Write $y = ab^x$ with **a and b values.**

Write the Equation of the graph. Write the Key Features.

1)

a:		b:	
Function/Equation:	$f(x) =$		

Exponential:	☐ Growth ☐ Decay
Ratio:	
$y - intercept$:	
Domain:	
Range:	
As $x \rightarrow \infty$	$y \rightarrow$
As $x \rightarrow -\infty$	$y \rightarrow$
Viable Solution:	Non − Viable:

2)

a:		b:	
Function/Equation:	$f(x) =$		

Exponential:	☐ Growth ☐ Decay
Ratio:	
$y - intercept$:	
Domain:	
Range:	
As $x \rightarrow \infty$	$y \rightarrow$
As $x \rightarrow -\infty$	$y \rightarrow$
Viable Solution:	Non − Viable:

3)

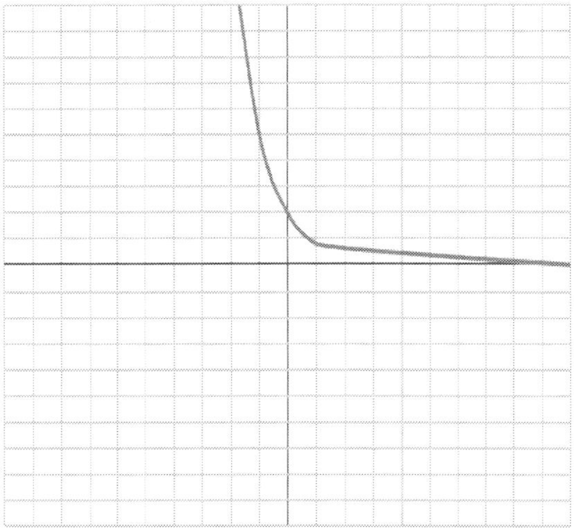

a:	b:
Function/Equation:	$f(x) =$

Exponential:	☐ Growth ☐ Decay
Ratio:	
$y - intercept$:	
Domain:	
Range:	
As $x \to \infty$	$y \to$
As $x \to -\infty$	$y \to$
Viable Solution:	Non − Viable:

4)

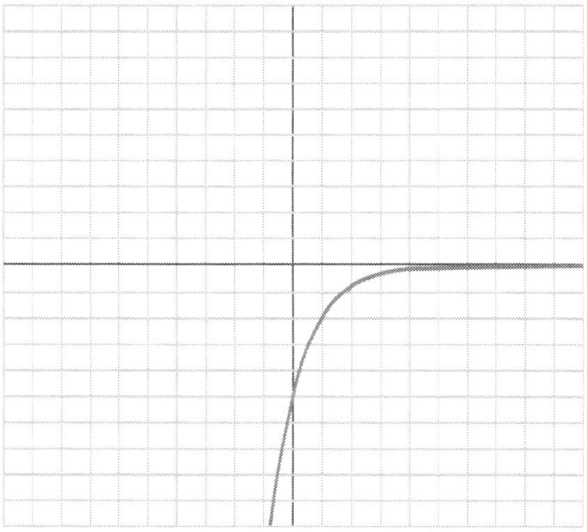

a:	b:
Function/Equation:	$f(x) =$

Exponential:	☐ Growth ☐ Decay
Ratio:	
$y - intercept$:	
Domain:	
Range:	
As $x \to \infty$	$y \to$
As $x \to -\infty$	$y \to$
Viable Solution:	Non − Viable:

 TEST TIME!

1) Select all of the key features of the Exponential function.

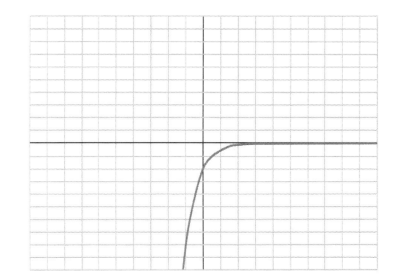

☐ $a = 2$

☐ $a = -2$

☐ $b = -4$

☐ $b = \frac{1}{4}$

☐ *This Function represents an Exponential Growth.*

☐ *This Function represents an Exponential Decay.*

☐ $f(x) = -2(\frac{1}{4})^x$ *represents the graph.*

☐ $f(x) = -2(4)^x$ *represents the graph.*

Unit 8 Lesson 5: Writing Exponential Equations Given a Table

MA.912.AR.5.3: Given a mathematical or real-world context, classify an exponential function as representing growth or decay.

MA.912.AR.5.4: Write an exponential function to represent a relationship between two quantities from a graph, a written description or a table of values within a mathematical or real-world context.

 SHOW US WHAT YOU KNOW!

1) Select all of the true statements about the function $y = -\frac{1}{2}(2)^x$

☐ It represents a linear function.

☐ It represents a quadratic function.

☐ It represents an Exponential function.

☐ Represents an Exponential Growth.

☐ Represents an Exponential Decay.

☐ (3,-4) is a viable solution.

☐ The common ratio is 2.

☐ The common ratio is $-\frac{1}{2}$.

☐ The initial value is 2.

☐ The initial value is $-\frac{1}{2}$.

BRAIN WORKOUT!
WRITE DOWN 4 EXAMPLES OF DIFFERENT EXPONENT PROPERTIES

STEPS TO WRITING AN EXPONENTIAL FUNCTION GIVEN A TABLE

GOAL: Write an exponential function given a table with key features.

1.	Find the **a = y-intercept = (0,y) or find the b = ratio/ pattern of the table** * If the table is increasing b>1 * If the table is decreasing b<1
2.	Plug in a or the b into $$y = ab^x$$
3.	Find a **viable solution** on the table **(x, y)** *Do not use the y-intercept again! *Try to use (1, y)
4.	Plug in Point **(x, y)** and **a** or **b** into $$y = ab^x.$$
5.	Solve for **a or b**. Use the Division Property of Equality, exponent laws, or the roots to cancel a or b and x.
6.	Write $y = ab^x$ with **a and b values.**

Use the table to write Exponential Equations.

1)

x	-1	0	2	3	4
y	-2	-4	−16	-32	-64

a:	b:
$Function/Equation$:	$f(x) =$

$Exponential$:	☐ $Growth$ ☐ $Decay$
$Ratio$:	
$y - intercept$:	
$Domain$:	
$Range$:	
$As\ x\ \to \infty$	$y \to$
$As\ x\ \to -\infty$	$y \to$
$Viable\ Solution$:	$Non - Viable$:

2)

x	-2	-1	0	1	2
$f(x)$	$\frac{1}{45}$	$\frac{1}{15}$	$\frac{1}{5}$	$\frac{3}{5}$	$\frac{9}{5}$

a:	b:
$Function/Equation$:	$f(x) =$

$Exponential$:	☐ $Growth$ ☐ $Decay$
$Ratio$:	
$y - intercept$:	
$Domain$:	
$Range$:	
$As\ x\ \to \infty$	$y \to$
$As\ x\ \to -\infty$	$y \to$
$Viable\ Solution$:	$Non - Viable$:

3)

x	-1	1	2	3	4
y	80	20	10	5	$\frac{5}{2}$

a:	b:
Function/Equation:	$f(x) =$

Exponential:	☐ Growth ☐ Decay
Ratio:	
$y - intercept$:	
Domain:	
Range:	
As $x \to \infty$	$y \to$
As $x \to -\infty$	$y \to$
Viable Solution:	Non − Viable:

4)

t	-2	-1	1	2	3
$g(t)$	-56	-28	-7	$\frac{-7}{2}$	$\frac{-7}{4}$

a:	b:
Function/Equation:	$f(x) =$

Exponential:	☐ Growth ☐ Decay
Ratio:	
$y - intercept$:	
Domain:	
Range:	
As $x \to \infty$	$y \to$
As $x \to -\infty$	$y \to$
Viable Solution:	Non − Viable:

 **TEST TIME!**

1) Select all of the key features of the table.

m	g(m)
-1	$\frac{2}{9}$
0	$\frac{2}{3}$
1	2
2	6
3	18

☐ $a = \frac{2}{9}$

☐ $a = \frac{2}{3}$

☐ $b = 3$

☐ $b = \frac{1}{3}$

☐ *This Function represents an Exponential Growth.*

☐ *This Function represents an Exponential Decay.*

☐ $f(x) = -3\left(\frac{2}{3}\right)^x$ *represents the graph.*

☐ $f(x) = \frac{2}{3}(3)^x$ *represents the graph.*

Unit 8 Lesson 6: Writing and Solving Exponential Equations Given a Real World

MA.912.AR.5.3: Given a mathematical or real-world context, classify an exponential function as representing growth or decay.

MA.912.AR.5.4: Write an exponential function to represent a relationship between two quantities from a graph, a written description or a table of values within a mathematical or real-world context.

MA.912.AR.5.6: Given a table, equation or written description of an exponential function, graph that function and determine its key features.

 SHOW US WHAT YOU KNOW!

1) Select all of the true statements about the function
$$y = -\frac{1}{2}x^2 + 4x - 2$$

☐ It represents a linear function.

☐ It represents a quadratic function.

☐ It represents an Exponential function.

☐ The axis of symmetry = $x = 4$.

☐ The axis of symmetry = $x = -4$.

☐ The Vertex = (4, 6)

☐ The Vertex = (4, -6)

☐ The initial value is 4.

☐ The initial value is -2.

BRAIN WORKOUT!
EXPONENTIAL FUNCTIONS AND WRITE WHAT EACH LETTER REPRESENTS:

VOCABULARY
EXPONENTIAL WORD PROBLEMS

# EXPONENTIAL GROWTH	**r = rate =** $\frac{\% \text{ of Increase}}{100}$ (Change percent to a decimal!) **ADD** 1 to the rate **a = initial amount = y-intercept** $$y = a(1 + r)^x$$
# EXPONENTIAL DECAY	**r = rate =** $\frac{\% \text{ of decrease}}{100}$ (Change percent to a decimal!) **SUBTRACT** 1 to the rate **a = initial amount = y-intercept** $$y = a(1 - r)^x$$
# b=RATIO=2	**Twice/doubled** $$y = a(2)^x$$
# b=RATIO=3	**Tripled** $$y = a(3)^x$$
# b=RATIO=1/2	**Half** $$y = a(\tfrac{1}{2})^x$$

Read each problem carefully and solve.

1) A town's population increases by 3% each year. This year, the population is at 53,478 people.

a) Write a function for this town's population. Use f(t) for the total population, after t years.	
b) What is the initial population?	
c) What is the Growth/Decay Factor?	% of Growth/Decay:
d) Exponential:	☐ Growth ☐ Decay
e) Approximately what is the population after 3 years?	
f) Draw a rough draft of what this would look like on an x, y chart.	

2) Trey has $40,000 in his savings account. He plans on taking half of his savings every 5 years to invest it.

a) Write a function for Trey. Use f(t) for the total amount in his savings account, after t years.	
b) What is the initial savings?	
c) What is the Growth/Decay Factor?	% of Growth/Decay:
d) Exponential:	☐ Growth ☐ Decay
e) Approximately how much does Trey have after 10 years?	
f) Draw a rough draft of what this would look like on an x, y chart.	

3) Rylan started with $480 in his savings account. Week 1 his savings increased exponentially to $513.60.	
a) Write a function for Rylan. Use f(x) for the total amount in his savings account, after x weeks.	
b) What is his initial savings?	
c) What is the Growth/Decay Factor?	% of Growth/Decay:
d) Exponential:	☐ Growth ☐ Decay
e) Approximately how much does Rylan have after 4 weeks?	
f) Draw a rough draft of what this would look like on an x, y chart.	

4) Ms. Cross purchased a car for $36,000. The car Depreciates by 6% each year.

a) Write a function for Ms. Cross. Use c(t) for the car's value, after t years.	
b) What is the initial amount?	
c) What is the Growth/Decay Factor?	% of Growth/Decay:
d) Exponential:	☐ Growth ☐ Decay
e) Approximately how much is the car worth after 7 years?	
f) Draw a rough draft of what this would look like on an x, y chart.	

5) Dr. Parks opened her own tutoring business. She started with 3 students and continued to grow by a factor of $\frac{1}{3}$ each month.	
a) Write a function for Dr. Parks. Use S(m) for the amount of students, after m months.	
b) What is the initial amount?	
c) What is the Growth/Decay Factor?	% of Growth/Decay:
d) Exponential:	☐ Growth ☐ Decay
e) Approximately how many students will Dr. Parks have after 5 months?	
f) Draw a rough draft of what this would look like on an x, y chart.	

TEST TIME!

1) Donna has $13,000 in her savings. She will triple her savings every 10 years.

☐ The initial is $13,000

☐ The initial is 10

☐ The ratio is 10

☐ The ratio is 3

☐ *This situation represents Exponential Growth.*

☐ *This situation represents an Exponential Decay.*

☐ $f(x) = 13,000(3)^{\frac{x}{10}}$ *represents the graph.*

☐ $f(x) = 13,000(1.3)^{\frac{x}{10}}$ *represents the graph.*

Unit 8 Lesson 7: Linear vs Exponential, Simple Interest vs Compound Interest

MA.912.FL.3.2: Solve real-world problems involving simple, compound and continuously compounded interest.

MA.912.AR.5.3: Given a mathematical or real-world context, classify an exponential function as representing growth or decay.

MA.912.AR.5.4: Write an exponential function to represent a relationship between two quantities from a graph, a written description or a table of values within a mathematical or real-world context.

MA.912.AR.5.6: Given a table, equation or written description of an exponential function, graph that function and determine its key features.

 **SHOW US WHAT YOU KNOW!**

1) Find the solution(s). Write solutions in simplified radical form.

$$y = -\frac{1}{2}x^2 + 4x - 2$$

BRAIN WORKOUT!

STEPS OF A LINE:

PARALLEL:

PERPENDICULAR:

DOMAIN:

RANGE:

X-INTERCEPT:

Y-INTERCEPT:

VOCABULARY
EXPONENTIAL WORD PROBLEMS

SIMPLE INTEREST/LINEAR	$A = P(1 + rt)$ or $I = prt$
	A = Final Amount **P =Initial Start value** **r = Annual Interest Rate** **t = time(in years)** | **I = Interest Earned** **P = Initial Start value** **r = Annual Interest rate** **t = time(in years)**

COMPOUND INTEREST/ EXPONENTIAL	$A = P(1 + \frac{r}{n})^{nt}$
	A = Final Amount **P = Initial Start Value** **r = Annual Interest Rate** **n = # of times interest is applied per year** **t = time (in years)**

Read each Problem carefully and solve. Round to the hundredth place.

1) Olivia has $400 in her savings account. The simple interest rate is 4% per year. How much will be in Olivia's account in 10 Years?

Principal	Interest	Rate	Time

2) Robby has $56,464 in his savings account. The interest rate is compounded monthly at 3.5%. How much will Robby have after 6 years?

Principal	Interest	Rate	Time	# of times per year

3) Cameron has $13,125.25 in her savings account. The interest rate is 3% compounded quarterly. How much will she have in 4 years?

Principal	Interest	Rate	Time	# of times per year

4) Ava has $12,000 in her savings account. The simple interest rate is 4.25% each year. How much will Ava have in 15 years?

Principal	Interest	Rate	Time

5) Taylor has $2500 in her savings account. It earns 4% interest, compounded every 3 months. How much interest did Taylor earn in the first year in her account after 5 years?

Principal	Interest	Rate	Time	# of times per year

6) Penelope is buying a car. She has $7000 saved and earns 2.5% each year. How much simple interest did Penelope earn in 3 years? Will she have enough to purchase a $10000 car?

Principal	Interest	Rate	Time

7) Marc has $5763 in his savings account. It earns 5.35% interest, compounded monthly. How much does Marc have in his account after 6 years?

Principal	Interest	Rate	Time	# of times per year

8) Andrew has $23715 in his savings account. It earns 2.7% interest, compounded monthly. How much does Andrew have in his account after 5 years?

Principal	Interest	Rate	Time	# of times per year

TEST TIME!

1) Donna has $13,000 in her savings. She earns 3% compounded monthly. Select all of the true statements.

☐ The Principal is $13,000

☐ The initial is 3

☐ The rate is 0.3

☐ The rate is 0.03

☐ $f(x) = 13,000(1 + \frac{0.03}{12})^{12t}$ *represents the graph.*

☐ $f(x) = 13,000(1 + \frac{0.3}{12})^{12t}$ *represents the graph.*

☐ In 10 years Donna will have approximately $17,541.60.

☐ In 10 years Donna will have approximately $251,655.95.

Unit 9 - Data Analysis		
1	Interpreting Data	161
2	Numerical Data	167
3	Categorical Data	172
4	Correlation Vs. Causation	176
5	Two-way Frequency Tables and Segmented Bar Graphs	179
6	Margin of Error	183

Unit 9 Lesson 1: Interpreting DATA

MA.912.DP.1.1: Given a set of data, select an appropriate method to represent the data, depending on whether it is numerical or categorical data and on whether it is univariate or bivariate.

MA.912.DP.1.2: Interpret data distributions represented in various ways. State whether the data is numerical or categorical, whether it is univariate or bivariate and interpret the different components and quantities in the display.

 SHOW US WHAT YOU KNOW!

1) The class averages on the math exams are 75, 53, 86, and 45. Ms. Mallek is giving one more test. She would like her total average to stay above a 70. What average MUST her class have on her next test in order for Ms. Mallek to achieve her goal?

BRAIN WORKOUT!
DEFINE:
LINEAR:

QUADRATIC:

CUBIC:

VOCABULARY

DATA	The collection of numerical or categorical statistics, that could be univariate or bivariate.
NUMERICAL DATA	Data collected in number form.
CATEGORICAL DATA	Data divided into groups.
UNIVARIATE DATA	One variable/type of data. Ex: Height of students
BIVARIATE DATA	Two variables/ two types of data. Ex: Height of students/ students who play sports
NUMERICAL UNIVARIATE DATA	Stem-and-Leaf Plots Histograms Line Plots/Dot Plots Box Plots
NUMERICAL BIVARIATE DATA	Scatter Plots Line Graphs
DISCRETE DATA	Data only takes certain numbers. Usually integers and whole numbers
CONTINUOUS DATA	Data could take any number as the input.
CATEGORICAL UNIVARIATE DATA	Circle Graphs Bar graphs Line Plots Frequency Tables Relative Frequency Tables
CATEGORICAL BIVARIATE DATA	Bar Charts Joint Frequency Tables Joint Relative Frequency Tables

CAUSATION	One change resulted because of another. Cause and Effect!
CORRELATION	One change is not necessarily the cause for another change. They correlate but NOT cause the Effect.

Small Numerical Data	Large Numerical Data	Categorical Data
Stem and Leaf Plot	**Histogram**	**Circle Graph**
Line Plot/Dot Plot	**Box Plot**	**Bar Graph**
Line Graph	**Scatter Plot**	

Classify each as Numerical or Categorical, Univariate or Bivariate. Then select which graph would be most appropriate for the Data.

1) Data on the SAT Scores of 10 students.
600, 750, 820, 870, 880, 1020, 1050, 1100, 1200, 1250

| ☐ Numerical | ☐ Univariate |
| ☐ Categorical | ☐ Bivariate |

☐ Box Plot	☐ Line Graph
☐ Histogram	☐ Stem-and-Leaf Plot
☐ Circle Graphs	
☐ Scatter Plots	☐ Dot Plot
☐ Bar Graphs	☐ Frequency Tables

2) Data on the number of people shopping and the temperature outside.

| ☐ Numerical | ☐ Univariate |
| ☐ Categorical | ☐ Bivariate |

☐ Box Plot	☐ Line Graph
☐ Histogram	☐ Stem-and-Leaf Plot
☐ Circle Graphs	
☐ Scatter Plots	☐ Dot Plot
☐ Bar Graphs	☐ Frequency Tables

3) Data on specific age and various theme parks

| ☐ Numerical | ☐ Univariate |
| ☐ Categorical | ☐ Bivariate |

☐ Box Plot	☐ Line Graph
☐ Histogram	☐ Stem-and-Leaf Plot
☐ Circle Graphs	
☐ Scatter Plots	☐ Dot Plot
☐ Bar Graphs	☐ Frequency Tables

4) Data on favorite subjects for students

| ☐ Numerical | ☐ Univariate |
| ☐ Categorical | ☐ Bivariate |

☐ Box Plot	☐ Line Graph
☐ Histogram	☐ Stem-and-Leaf Plot
☐ Circle Graphs	
☐ Scatter Plots	☐ Dot Plot
☐ Bar Graphs	☐ Frequency Tables

5) Data on Student Siblings

| ☐ Numerical | ☐ Univariate |
| ☐ Categorical | ☐ Bivariate |

☐ Box Plot	☐ Line Graph
☐ Histogram	☐ Stem-and-Leaf Plot
☐ Circle Graph	
☐ Scatter Plots	☐ Dot Plot
☐ Bar Graphs	☐ Frequency Tables

6) Data on Favorite Ice cream Flavor

| ☐ Numerical | ☐ Univariate |
| ☐ Categorical | ☐ Bivariate |

☐ Box Plot	☐ Line Graph
☐ Histogram	☐ Stem-and-Leaf Plot
☐ Circle Graph	
☐ Scatter Plots	☐ Dot Plot
☐ Bar Graphs	☐ Frequency Tables

7) The number of people at the fair on Saturday vs. Tuesday	8) The number of people at the fair on Saturday if it rains or is sunny.
☐ Numerical ☐ Univariate ☐ Categorical ☐ Bivariate ☐ Box Plot ☐ Line Graph ☐ Histogram ☐ Stem-and-Leaf Plot ☐ Circle Graph ☐ Scatter Plots ☐ Dot Plot ☐ Bar Graphs ☐ Frequency Tables	☐ Numerical ☐ Univariate ☐ Categorical ☐ Bivariate ☐ Box Plot ☐ Line Graph ☐ Histogram ☐ Stem-and-Leaf Plot ☐ Circle Graph ☐ Scatter Plots ☐ Dot Plot ☐ Bar Graphs ☐ Frequency Tables

Classify each Data chart as Numerical or Categorical	
1) Line Plot/Dot Plot	2) Circle Graph
3) Histogram	4) Box plot
5)Stem-and-Leaf Plot	6) Line Graph

1) For which data should a histogram be used. Select all that apply.

☐ Daily temperature for a year

☐ Students Height in a class

☐ Students Height in a school

☐ Students favorite ice cream

☐ Students averages in a math class

☐ Student scores on the state exam

Unit 9 Lesson 2: Numerical Data

MA.912.DP.1.1: Given a set of data, select an appropriate method to represent the data, depending on whether it is numerical or categorical data and on whether it is univariate or bivariate.

MA.912.DP.1.2: Interpret data distributions represented in various ways. State whether the data is numerical or categorical, whether it is univariate or bivariate and interpret the different components and quantities in the display.

MA.912.DP.1.4: Estimate a population total, mean or percentage using data from a sample survey; develop a margin of error through the use of simulation.

 SHOW US WHAT YOU KNOW!

1) Select all of the data that would be classified as Numerical Univariate

☐ Height of dogs

☐ Weight of dogs

☐ Ice cream Flavor

☐ Number of people shopping when store has a sale

☐ Student siblings

☐ Zip Code

BRAIN WORKOUT!
STEPS OF A LINE:

PARALLEL:

PERPENDICULAR:

DOMAIN:

RANGE:

X-INTERCEPT:

Y-INTERCEPT:

Measure of Center

Normal Data (No Outliers)	Skewed Data (Outliers)
Mean: Average- add data values and divide by # of data values <ul><li>BELL CURVE</li><li>NO OUTLIERS</li><li>Standard Deviation for the Spread</li></ul>	Median: List data values in order from least to greatest. Find middle #. If 2 values in the middle take the mean of the 2 data values. <ul><li>Used when data has OUTLIERS</li><li>SKEWED DATA</li><li>Interquartile Range for the Spread</li></ul>

Measure of Variation

Normal Data (No Outliers)	Skewed Data (Outliers)
Range: High data value- low data value <ul><li>BELL CURVE</li><li>NO OUTLIERS</li></ul>	Interquartile Range: Quartile 3-Quartile 1 <ul><li>Used when data has OUTLIERS</li><li>SKEWED DATA</li></ul>

Compare the two dot plots and answer each section.

1)

Funeas' Test Grade (dot plot, Frequency vs Test Grades)

Mallek's Test Grade (dot plot, Frequency vs Test Grades)

☐ Normal Data/Bell Curve
☐ Skewed Data

☐ Normal Data/Bell Curve
☐ Skewed Data

Mean:	Median:	Mean:	Median:

Most appropriate measure of spread/Variation ☐ Range/Standard Deviation ☐ Interquartile Range	Most appropriate measure of center ☐ Mean ☐ Median	Most appropriate measure of spread/Variation ☐ Range/Standard Deviation ☐ Interquartile Range	Most appropriate measure of center ☐ Mean ☐ Median
Create a box plot		Create a box plot	

2)		DATA 1: ☐ Normal Data/Bell Curve ☐ Skewed Data	DATA 2: ☐ Normal Data/Bell Curve ☐ Skewed Data
Data 1 Minimum: Maximum: Quartile 1: Quartile 3: Median:	**Data 2** Minimum: Maximum: Quartile 1: Quartile 3: Median:	Data 1 Interquartile Range: Data 1 Range:	Data 2 Interquartile Range: Data 2 Range:
Data 1: Most appropriate measure of spread/Variation ☐ Range/Standard Deviation ☐ Interquartile Range	Data 1: Most appropriate measure of center ☐ Mean ☐ Median	Data 2: Most appropriate measure of spread/Variation ☐ Range/Standard Deviation ☐ Interquartile Range	Data 2: Most appropriate measure of center ☐ Mean ☐ Median

TEST TIME!

1) Select all the true statements about the data.

☐ Data is Normal
   distribution

☐ Data is skewed right

☐ Data has an outlier

☐ Quartile 3 is 55

☐ Median is 60

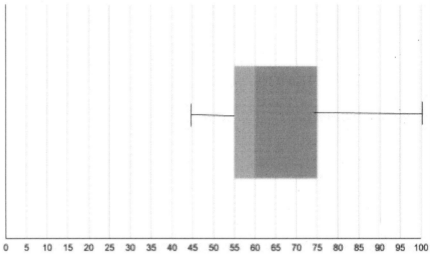

0 5 10 15 20 25 30 35 40 45 50 55 60 65 70 75 80 85 90 95 100

☐ Interquartile Range
   is the appropriate spread for the data

☐ Standard Deviation is the appropriate spread for the data

☐ Mean is 60

Unit 9 Lesson 3: Categorical Data

MA.912.DP.1.1: Given a set of data, select an appropriate method to represent the data, depending on whether it is numerical or categorical data and on whether it is univariate or bivariate.

MA.912.DP.1.2: Interpret data distributions represented in various ways. State whether the data is numerical or categorical, whether it is univariate or bivariate and interpret the different components and quantities in the display.

MA.912.DP.1.4: Estimate a population total, mean or percentage using data from a sample survey; develop a margin of error through the use of simulation.

 SHOW US WHAT YOU KNOW!

1) Write the function in vertex form.

$$f(x) = -x^2 - 6x + 3$$

BRAIN WORKOUT!
DEFINE:
Polynomial:

Monomial:

Binomial:

Trinomial:

Observe each graph. Answer each question carefully.

120 students were surveyed on their favorite animal.

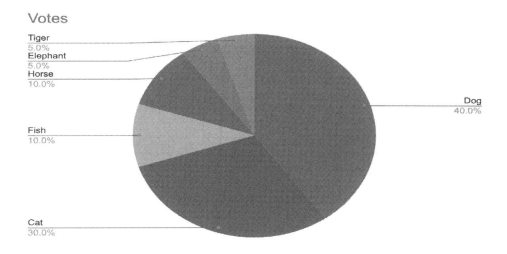

Votes

Tiger 5.0%
Elephant 5.0%
Horse 10.0%
Fish 10.0%
Dog 40.0%
Cat 30.0%

1) Which animal was the least favorite?	2) Which animal had the most votes?
3) How many students voted for Elephants?	4) How many students voted for fish?
5) How many students voted for dogs?	6) How many students voted for cats?

Students were surveyed on their favorite ice cream flavor.

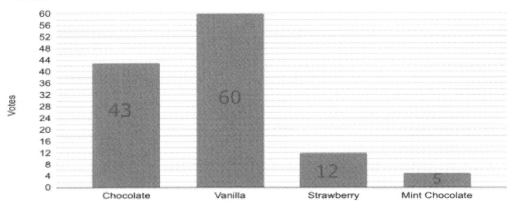

7) What percentage of students preferred strawberry flavored ice cream?

8) What percentage of students preferred vanilla flavored ice cream?

9) What was the students least favorite ice cream flavor?

10) What percentage of students preferred Mint Chocolate flavored ice cream?

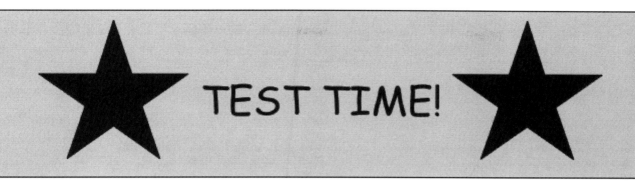

TEST TIME!

1) 300 students were surveyed on their favorite color. Select all the true statements about the survey.

☐ 6 students voted yellow

☐ 2 students voted yellow

☐ 114 students voted red

☐ Blue had the most votes

☐ 47 students voted for blue

☐ More than ½ the students vote for red

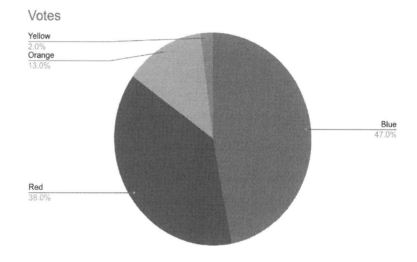

Votes

Yellow 2.0%
Orange 13.0%
Blue 47.0%
Red 38.0%

Unit 9 Lesson 4: Correlation vs. Causation

MA.912.DP.1.3: Explain the difference between correlation and causation in the contexts of both numerical and categorical data.

 **SHOW US WHAT YOU KNOW!**

1) List the key features of the function: $f(x) = -|x - 3| + 5$

Maximum/Minimum:	
Axis of Symmetry:	
Vertex:	
Rate of change:	
x-intercept(s):	
y-intercept:	
Domain:	
Range:	
End Behavior: $x \to \infty,$ $x \to -\infty$	$y \to$ $y \to$

BRAIN WORKOUT!
EXPONENTIAL FUNCTIONS AND WRITE WHAT EACH LETTER REPRESENTS:

Select if each scenario has a correlation, causation, or both.

1) Eating healthy makes you exercise more.

- ☐ Positive correlation
- ☐ Negative correlation
- ☐ Causation
- ☐ Both Correlation and Causation
- ☐ Neither

2) Drinking more soda you absorb more sugar.

- ☐ Positive correlation
- ☐ Negative correlation
- ☐ Causation
- ☐ Both Correlation and Causation
- ☐ Neither

3) Having a test, hours studying the night before.

- ☐ Positive correlation
- ☐ Negative correlation
- ☐ Causation
- ☐ Both Correlation and Causation
- ☐ Neither

4) More people at the restaurant, more food to purchase for the restaurant.

- ☐ Positive correlation
- ☐ Negative correlation
- ☐ Causation
- ☐ Both Correlation and Causation
- ☐ Neither

5) Bad reviews on a movie less people watch the movie

- ☐ Positive correlation
- ☐ Negative correlation
- ☐ Causation
- ☐ Both Correlation and Causation
- ☐ Neither

6) It is cold outside, so more people stay in their homes

- ☐ Positive correlation
- ☐ Negative correlation
- ☐ Causation
- ☐ Both Correlation and Causation
- ☐ Neither

7) Studying for a math test. Taking my dog out for a walk.

- ☐ Positive correlation
- ☐ Negative correlation
- ☐ Causation
- ☐ Both Correlation and Causation
- ☐ Neither

8) I go for a jog, I am physically tired.

- ☐ Positive correlation
- ☐ Negative correlation
- ☐ Causation
- ☐ Both Correlation and Causation
- ☐ Neither

1) Select all the true statements about the scenario. My clothes are dirty, so I wash my clothes.

☐ Positive correlation

☐ Negative correlation

☐ Causation

☐ Both Correlation and Causation

☐ Neither

Unit 9 Lesson 5: Two- Way Frequency Tables and Segmented Bar Graphs.

MA.912.DP.3.1: Construct a two-way frequency table summarizing bivariate categorical data. Interpret joint and marginal frequencies and determine possible associations in terms of a real-world context.

 SHOW US WHAT YOU KNOW!

1) List the key features of the function: $f(x) = (2x + 6)(x - 1)$

Maximum/Minimum:	
Axis of Symmetry:	
Vertex:	
x-intercept(s):	
y-intercept:	
Domain:	
Range:	
End Behavior: $x \to \infty,$ $x \to -\infty$	$y \to$ $y \to$

BRAIN WORKOUT!
STEPS OF A LINE:

PARALLEL:

PERPENDICULAR:

DOMAIN:

RANGE:

X-INTERCEPT:

Y-INTERCEPT:

Fill out the Frequency Tables. Answer the questions that follow.

1) Dr. Parks took a survey and asked all 130, 9th and 10th grade students, which class they love to attend, Algebra, English, Science, or Social Studies. Of the 65 10th graders, 24 preferred Algebra. 25 of her students chose English and 53 total for Algebra. 12 9th graders preferred English and 20 10th graders preferred Social Studies. Only 9 9th graders preferred science. Fill in the Two- Way Frequency table and answer the questions.

	Algebra	English	Science	Social Studies	Total
9th Graders					
10th Graders					
Total					

2) What is the largest Marginal Frequency?

3) What is the largest Joint Frequency?

4) How many students prefer Social Studies?

5) What is the % of students who are 9th graders who prefer Science?

6) What is the percentage of students who prefer Algebra?

7) What is the probability of a student being a 10th grader who prefers English?

8) Students in math classes at a local high school were surveyed on which pet they prefer, Dog, Cat, Bunny, or Reptile. The results are shown in the two-way frequency table and the segmented Bar graph.

	9th Graders	10th Graders	11th Graders	Total
Dog	161	29	26	216
Cat	48	62	16	126
Bunny	12	3	0	15
Reptile	32	93	5	130
Total	253	187	47	487

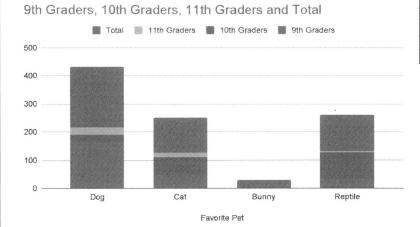

9th Graders, 10th Graders, 11th Graders and Total

■ Total ■ 11th Graders ■ 10th Graders ■ 9th Graders

Favorite Pet

9) Label the Marginal Frequency on the table.

10) Label the Joint Frequency on the table.

11) How many students prefer dogs?

12) What is the % of students who are 9th graders who prefer a bunny?

13) What is the percentage of students who prefer reptiles?

14) What is the probability of a student being an 11th grader who prefers a cat?

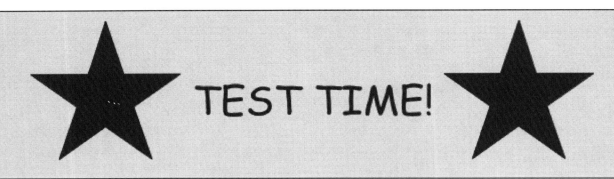

TEST TIME!

1) Ms. Irwin took a survey and asked all 127, 9th and 10th grade students, which sport they enjoy playing the most. Of the 65 10th graders, 24 preferred Basketball. 25 of her students chose Baseball and 30 total for Soccer. 12 9th graders preferred football and 20 10th graders preferred football. Only 9 9th graders preferred baseball. Fill in the Two- Way Frequency table. Label the Marginal frequency. Label the Joint Frequency.

	Football	Baseball	Soccer	Basketball	Total
9th Graders					
10th Graders					
Total					

Unit 9 Lesson 6: Margin of Error

MA.912.DP.1.4: Estimate a population total, mean or percentage using data from a sample survey; develop a margin of error through the use of simulation.

 **SHOW US WHAT YOU KNOW!**

1) List the key features of the function: $y = \frac{3}{4}(x - 4)^2$

Maximum/Minimum:	
Axis of Symmetry:	
Vertex:	
x-intercept(s):	
y-intercept:	
Domain:	
Range:	
End Behavior: $x \to \infty,$ $x \to -\infty$	$y \to$ $y \to$

BRAIN WORKOUT!

STEPS OF A QUADRATIC:

Answer the questions that follow the graph.

1) A survey was taken from a group of elementary students asking what their favorite animal is. The results are shown in the circle graph below with a margin of error of 2.5%. There were 745 students in the school.

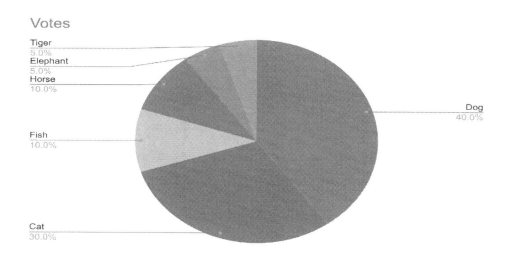

2) According to the survey, what would be the estimated students who voted cat as their favorite animal?

3) According to the survey, what would be the maximum number of students who voted Dog as their favorite animal?

4) According to the survey, what would be the minimum number of students who voted tiger as their favorite animal?

5) According to the survey, what would be the range of students who voted horse as their favorite animal?

Answer each question carefully.

6) A survey was given to 325 people asking what they enjoy doing on the weekends. 18% of the people who voted said watch tv, 27% said go to the beach, 55% said play sports. The margin of error for this survey was 3%.

7) According to the survey, what would be the estimated # of people who enjoy watching tv on the weekends?

8) If another survey was given, but this time with 500 people, how many would enjoy playing sports on the weekend?

9) According to the survey, what would be the minimum number of people who enjoy going to the beach on the weekend?

10) According to the survey, what would be the range of people who enjoyed going to the beach on the weekend?

TEST TIME!

1) Ms. Irwin took a survey and asked all 127 students which subject they liked the most. The results were, 48% said math, 29% said history, 10% said reading, and 13% said science. GO MATH! The margin of error was 1.5%. What would be the range of students who voted for math?

Unit 10 - Function Review

Unit 10 Lesson 1: Comparing Linear, Quadratic and Exponential Functions

MA.912.F.1.1: Given an equation or graph that defines a function, determine the function type. Given an input-output table, determine a function type that could represent it.

MA.912.F.1.6: Compare key features of linear and nonlinear functions each represented algebraically, graphically, in tables or written descriptions.

MA.912.F.1.8: Determine whether a linear, quadratic or exponential function best models a given real-world situation.

 SHOW US WHAT YOU KNOW!

1) Write the viable solution to the system

$-2x + 5y = 21$

$-x = 2y + 6$

BRAIN WORKOUT!
EXPONENTIAL FUNCTIONS AND WRITE WHAT EACH LETTER REPRESENTS:

VOCABULARY

Function	For every input there is exactly one output. The x values cannot repeat!
Linear Function	A function that creates a straight line. Degree = Largest exponent on variable = 1 **1) Slope = Constant Rate of Change =** $$m = \frac{y_2 - y_1}{x_2 - x_1}$$ **2) Point-Slope Form:** $y - y_1 = m(x - x_1)$ **3) Slope-Intercept Form:** $y = mx + b$ **4) Standard Form:** $Ax + By = C$
Quadratic Function	A function that creates a parabola. Degree = Largest exponent on variable = 2 **1) Standard Form:** $$y = ax^2 + bx \boxed{+ c} \; \text{←} \quad \text{Y-intercept} \\ \text{Initial value}$$

To Find Vertex:	
Axis of symmetry: $x = h = \frac{-b}{2a}$	**Plug in x to get y=k** **This is your range**

2) Quadratic Formula:
$$x = \frac{-b \pm \sqrt{b^2 - 4ac}}{2a} = p \; and \; q$$

3) Vertex Form: $y = a(x - h)^2 + k$
    (h, k) = Vertex

4) Factored Form: $y = a(x - p)(x - q)$
    p and q represent x-intercepts

To Find Vertex:	
Axis of symmetry: $x = h = \frac{p+q}{2}$	**Plug in x to get y=k** **This is your range**

Absolute Value

1) **Vertex Form:**

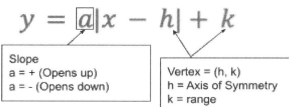

$$y = \boxed{a}|x - h| + k$$

Slope
a = + (Opens up)
a = - (Opens down)

Vertex = (h, k)
h = Axis of Symmetry
k = range

2) X-intercepts

5) Plug 0 into y
6) Isolate the Absolute value on one side

One Solution:	Two Solutions:	No Solution:
| | = 0	| | = +	| | = −

Exponential Function

1) **Standard Form:**

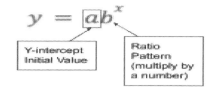

$$y = \boxed{a}\boxed{b}^x$$

Y-intercept
Initial Value

Ratio
Pattern
(multiply by a number)

2) **Exponential Growth with %:**

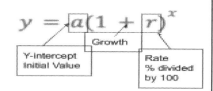

$$y = \boxed{a}(1 + \boxed{r})^x$$

Growth

Y-intercept
Initial Value

Rate
% divided by 100

3) **Exponential Decay with %:**

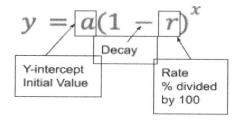

$$y = \boxed{a}(1 - \boxed{r})^x$$

Decay

Y-intercept
Initial Value

Rate
% divided by 100

X-INTERCEPT	(x,0) Plug in 0 into y
Y-INTERCEPT	(0,y) Plug in 0 into X
DOMAIN **X**	Set of inputs in the function. The independent variable. Time
RANGE $Y=f(x)$	Set of outputs in the function. The dependent variable. Total once you input x value.
VIABLE	The inputs and outputs satisfy the functions constraints.
NON -VIABLE	The inputs and outputs DO NOT satisfy the functions constraints.

Function	Key Words
LINEAR	per, each, every, constant rate of change, adding or subtracting by a constant #, simple interest
QUADRATIC	maximum, minimum, vertex, increasing interval, decreasing interval, ground, solutions, roots, zeros
EXPONENTIAL	double, triple, quadruple, multiplying or dividing by a common ratio, compound interest, percent of increase, percent of decrease
ABSOLUTE VALUE	tolerance, fluctuate, range, maximum, minimum

Write the key features of each function and compare them with the other functions. Circle the function with the largest x-intercept, and y-intercept.

$2x + 4y = 8$	$y = (2x - 4)(x + 2)$	$y = \frac{1}{2}|x - 5| + 3$	$y = 2(1 - 0.43)^x$
Function:	Function:	Function:	Function:
x-intercept(s):	x-intercept(s):	x-intercept(s):	x-intercept(s):
y-intercept:	y-intercept:	y-intercept:	y-intercept:
Left End Behavior:	axis of symmetry:	axis of symmetry:	Growth or Decay:
Right End Behavior:	Vertex:	Vertex:	Common Ratio:
Slope:	Maximum or Minimum Value:	Slope:	Percent of growth or decay:
Domain:	Domain:	Domain:	Domain:
Range:	Range:	Range:	Range:

x	f(x)
0	4
1	5
2	4
3	3

x	g(x)
-1	-4
0	-5
1	-4
2	-1

x	h(x)
1	9
2	6
3	3
4	0

x	t(x)
-1	2
0	4
1	8
2	16

Function:	Function:	Function:	Function:
x-intercept(s):	x-intercept(s):	x-intercept(s):	x-intercept(s):
y-intercept:	y-intercept:	y-intercept:	y-intercept:
axis of symmetry:	axis of symmetry:	Left End Behavior:	Growth or Decay:
Vertex:	Vertex:	Right End Behavior:	Common Ratio:
Slope:	Maximum or Minimum Value:	Slope:	Percent of growth or decay:
Domain:	Domain:	Domain:	Domain:
Range:	Range:	Range:	Range:

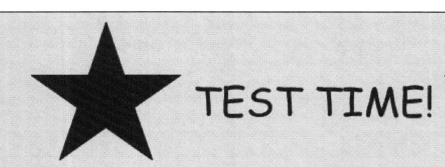 

TEST TIME!

1) Which equation has the larger x-intercept?

$y - 2 = \frac{4}{5}(x + 5)$	$y = 12x^2 + 12x + 3$

Unit 10 Lesson 2: Parent Functions

MA.912.F.1.1: Given an equation or graph that defines a function, determine the function type. Given an input-output table, determine a function type that could represent it.

MA.912.F.1.6: Compare key features of linear and nonlinear functions each represented algebraically, graphically, in tables or written descriptions.

MA.912.F.1.8: Determine whether a linear, quadratic or exponential function best models a given real-world situation.

 SHOW US WHAT YOU KNOW!

1) Nikie is starting her own candle company. She needs to purchase supplies for each candle. Each candle will cost her $2.34. She plans on selling each candle for $7.00. If she purchases supplies for 20 candles how much money will Nikie profit?

BRAIN WORKOUT!

Define:
Polynomial:

Monomial:

Binomial:

Trinomial:

Graph the key features of each parent function and compare them with the other functions.

1) $y = x$

Parent Function:

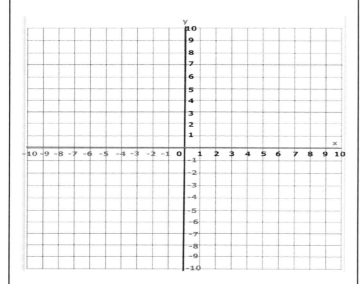

2) $y = x^2$

Parent Function:

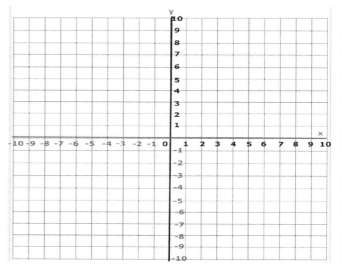

3) $y = |x|$

Parent Function:

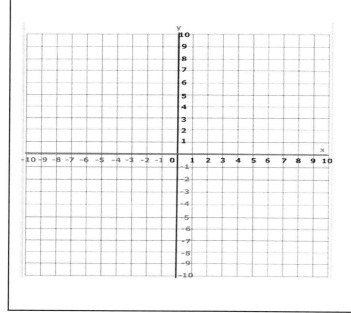

4) $y = 2^x$

Parent Function:

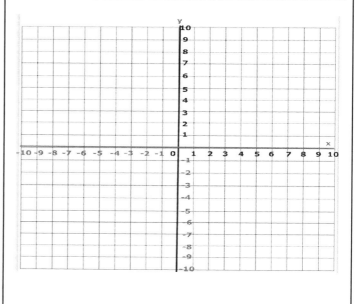

5) $y = \frac{1}{2}^x$

Parent Function:

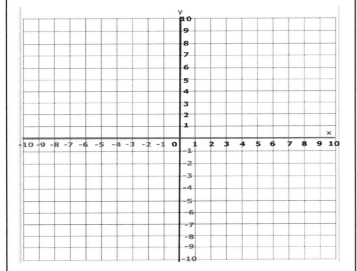

6) $y = x^3$

Parent Function:

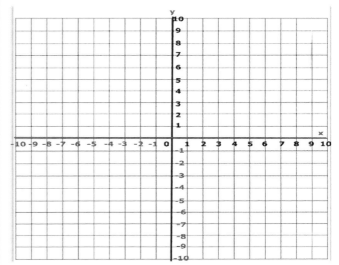

7) $y = \sqrt{x}$

Parent Function:

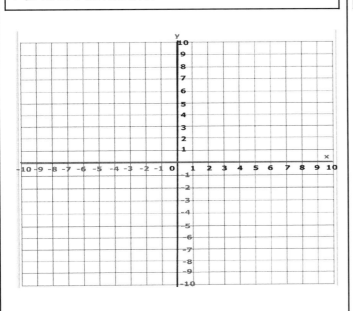

8) $y = \sqrt[3]{x}$

Parent Function:

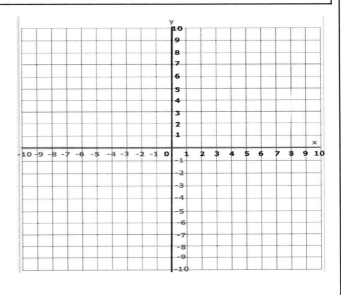

Match the transformation table with the correct parent function:

9)

x	y
2	-4
3	-3
4	-4
5	-7

x	y
0	-3
1	2
3	12
4	17

x	y
-2	27
-1	9
0	3
1	1

x	y
0	8
1	6
2	8
3	10

☐ Linear

☐ Quadratic

☐ $y = x^3$

☐ $y = |x|$

☐ $y = 2^x$

☐ Exponential Decay

☐ Square Root

TEST TIME!

1) Which parent function does this transformation belong to?

$$y - 7 + x = 2(3x + 5)$$

Unit 10 Lesson 3: Transformation of Functions

MA.912.F.2.1: Identify the effect on the graph or table of a given function after replacing *f(x)* by *f(x)+k,kf(x)*, *f(kx)* and *f(x+k)* for specific values of *k*.

MA.912.F.1.1: Given an equation or graph that defines a function, determine the function type. Given an input-output table, determine a function type that could represent it.

MA.912.F.1.6: Compare key features of linear and nonlinear functions each represented algebraically, graphically, in tables or written descriptions.

MA.912.F.1.8: Determine whether a linear, quadratic or exponential function best models a given real-world situation.

 SHOW US WHAT YOU KNOW!

1) Concert tickets for adults are $85 each and for children they are $65 each. The venue made $53,125 in ticket sales. They sold 725 tickets altogether. How many adult tickets were sold at the concert?

BRAIN WORKOUT!
Define:
LINEAR:

QUADRATIC:

CUBIC:

Transformations

Vertical		Horizontal	
$f(x)+k$	Shifts the Parent graph **up** k units	$f(x+k)$	Shifts the Parent graph **left** k units
$f(x)-k$	Shifts the Parent graph **down** k units	$f(x-k)$	Shifts the Parent graph **right** k units
$kf(x)$, $\|k\| > 1$	Vertical **Stretch**	$f(kx)$, $0 < \|k\| < 1$	Horizontal **Stretch**
$kf(x)$, $0 < \|k\| < 1$	Vertical Shrink Vertical **Compression**	$f(kx)$, $\|k\| > 1$	Horizontal Shrink Horizontal **Compression**

Reflection

$-f(x)$	Over y-axis	$f(-x)$	Over x-axis

Write the transformed function equation according to the description. Graph and label both the parent and transformation graph.

1)

Parent:
$f(x) = |x|$

Transform 3 units to the left

☐ Vertical Shift

☐ Horizontal Shift

Transformation Function:

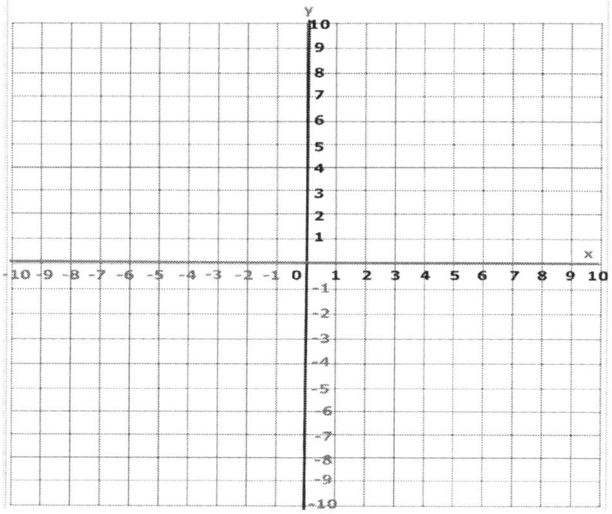

2)

Parent:
$f(x) = x$

Transform 5 units up

☐ Vertical Shift

☐ Horizontal Shift

Transformation Function:

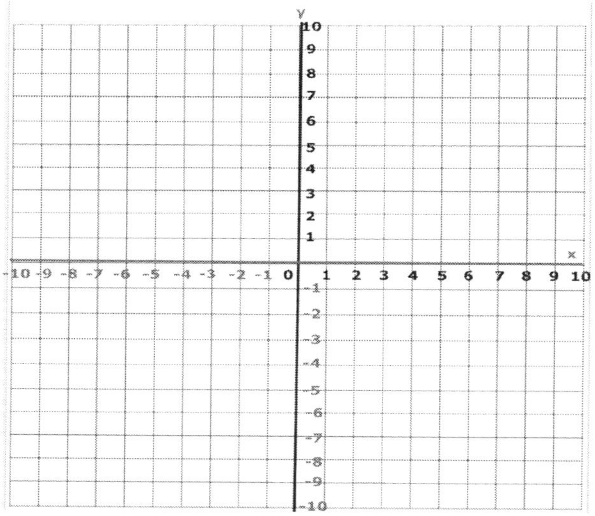

3)

Parent:
$f(x) = \frac{1}{2}^{x}$

Transformation
Function:

**Transform 4
units down**

☐ Vertical Shift

☐ Horizontal
Shift

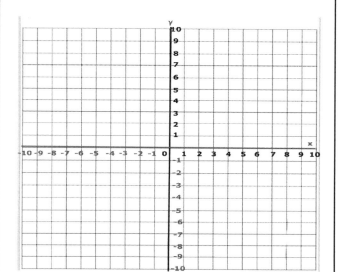

4)

Parent:
$f(x) = x^2$

Transformation
Function:

**Transform 1 unit
to the right.**

☐ Vertical Shift

☐ Horizontal
Shift

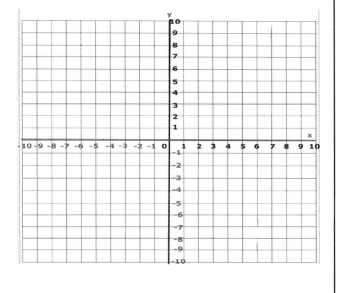

Write the transformation function according to the description.

5)

Parent:
$f(x) = x^2$

Transformation Function:

Transform 1 unit to the right. 2 units up. Reflect over the x axis. Compress vertically by 1/2.

☐ Vertical Shift

☐ Horizontal Shift

6)

Parent:
$f(x) = |x|$

Transformation Function:

Transform 1 unit to the left. 2 units down. Reflect over the x axis.

☐ Vertical Shift

☐ Horizontal Shift

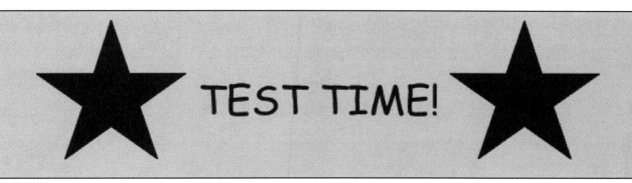

TEST TIME!

1) Complete the statement: Use the word bank given.

The function $f(x) = -|x + 3| - 4$ is a transformation of the parent

_____ function. This function has a horizontal shift of

_____ units to the _____. This function also has a vertical shift of

_____ units _____. This function is reflected over the _____ axis.

Word Bank:			
Quadratic	Exponential	Cubic	Absolute Value
Linear	three	four	five
Up	down	left	right
x	y		

Unit 10 Lesson 4: Interpret Equations and Expressions

MA.912.AR.1.1: Identify and interpret parts of an equation or expression that represent a quantity in terms of a mathematical or real-world context, including viewing one or more of its parts as a single entity.

MA.912.F.1.1: Given an equation or graph that defines a function, determine the function type. Given an input-output table, determine a function type that could represent it.

MA.912.F.1.6: Compare key features of linear and nonlinear functions each represented algebraically, graphically, in tables or written descriptions.

MA.912.F.1.8: Determine whether a linear, quadratic or exponential function best models a given real-world situation.

 SHOW US WHAT YOU KNOW!

1) A ball is thrown from a 25 foot building. The maximum height of the ball is reached in 4 seconds at 30 feet. Use h(t) for the height of the ball and let t represent the seconds. Write a function in standard form.

BRAIN WORKOUT!
WRITE 5 RATIONAL SQUARE ROOTS AND 5 RATIONAL CUBE ROOTS

VOCABULARY

TERM	A number or variable or both. Ex: 7, x, 7x
LEADING TERM	When the polynomial is in standard form it is the first term. The term with the highest degree Ex: Leading term = $2x^3$ $3x^2 - x + 1 + 2x^3$
COEFFICIENT	The number that is multiplied by a variable(s) Ex: The coefficient = 2 $2x^3 y$
LEADING COEFFICIENT	The coefficient of the term with the largest degree. Ex: Leading coefficient = 2 $3x^2 - x + 1 + 2x^3$
VARIABLE	A letter representing a number Ex: x, y, z
CONSTANT	The number without a variable. Ex: The constant = 1 $7x^3 + 3x^2 - x + 1$
EQUATION	When 2 expressions are equivalent in math Ex: 2x=8
EXPRESSION	Has letters, numbers, and at least one operation. Ex: 2x+3

Identify and interpret each part of the expressions, equations, and functions.

1) 37x+53y+128z

Terms:	
Type of Polynomial:	
Coefficients:	
Constant:	
Represents a:	☐ Equation ☐ Expression ☐ Function

2) $f(x)=\frac{1}{2}x + 5$

Terms:	
Type of Function:	
Coefficients:	
Constant:	
Represents a:	☐ Equation ☐ Expression ☐ Function

3) Emilly purchased movie tickets for her family. Kid tickets are $7.50 each and adult Tickets are $12.50 each. She spent $47.50.

7.50k+12.50a=47.50 Represent a:	☐ Equation ☐ Expression ☐ Function

If Emilly bought a total of 5 tickets how many kid and adult tickets did she purchase?

4) The area of a rectangular backyard is 800 feet. The length is twice the length of the width.

l=2w	☐ Equation ☐ Expression ☐ Function
A=l*w	☐ Equation ☐ Expression ☐ Function

Find the Length of the backyard.

5) The function $f(t) = 13500(1 + 0.037)^t$ represents the population of a city, t years, since 2005.

Type of Function:	
Represents a:	☐ Growth ☐ Decay
Population in 2005:	
% of growth Growth rate:	
Ratio:	
Population in 2023:	

6) The perimeter of a classroom is 160 feet. The length of the room is 3 times the size of the width.

p=2l+2w	☐ Equation ☐ Expression ☐ Function
l=3w	☐ Equation ☐ Expression ☐ Function

Find the length and width of the classroom.

7) Laura bought a new car and was told the function $f(x) = 45,389(0.97)^x$ represents the car's value.

x represents:	
f(x) represents:	
45,389 represents:	
0.97 represents:	
% rate of change:	
What is Laura's car worth after 7 years?	

8) Michael is signing up for camp. They are offering 1 discounted day for $12 and $20 for each additional day you attend camp. The expression $20(x - 1) + 12$ represents the total Michael will spend at camp.

x represents:	
20 represents:	
(x-1) represents:	
20(x-1) represents:	
12 represents:	

1) The equation $y = -2(x - 3)^2 + 32$, represents the height of a diver, diving from a diving board. Fill in the table.

Type of Function:	
x represents:	
y represents:	
32 represents:	
3 represents:	
Initial Height of the Diver:	
How long does it take the diver to hit the water?	

Unit 10 Lesson 5: Real World Functions

MA.912.AR.1.1: Identify and interpret parts of an equation or expression that represent a quantity in terms of a mathematical or real-world context, including viewing one or more of its parts as a single entity.

MA.912.F.1.1: Given an equation or graph that defines a function, determine the function type. Given an input-output table, determine a function type that could represent it.

MA.912.F.1.6: Compare key features of linear and nonlinear functions each represented algebraically, graphically, in tables or written descriptions.

MA.912.F.1.8: Determine whether a linear, quadratic or exponential function best models a given real-world situation.

 SHOW US WHAT YOU KNOW!

1) Fill in the table with the key features of the function:

$y = 3(0.87)^x$

x-intercept:	
y-intercept:	
Ratio:	
% rate of change:	
Growth ☐ yes ☐ no	Decay ☐ yes ☐ no
Asymptote:	
Domain:	
Range:	
End Behavior: $x \to \infty$, $x \to -\infty$	$y \to$ $y \to$

BRAIN WORKOUT!
KEYWORDS TO LOOK FOR IN A WORD PROBLEM FOR A LINE

Function	Key Words
LINEAR	per, each, every, constant rate of change, adding or subtracting by a constant #, simple interest
QUADRATIC	maximum, minimum, vertex, increasing interval, decreasing interval, ground, solutions, roots, zeros
EXPONENTIAL	double, triple, quadruple, multiplying or dividing by a common ratio, compound interest, percent of increase, percent of decrease
ABSOLUTE VALUE	tolerance, fluctuate, range, maximum, minimum

Complete the table for each real world scenario.

1) Buying a car at 47,800 and it depreciates each year by 3.25%.

Function Type:	
Function:	
x-intercept:	
y-intercept:	
Ratio:	
Cost of the car in 10 years?	

2) A gym charges an initial registration fee of $80 and it is $23 for each additional month.

Function Type:	
Function:	
x-intercept:	
y-intercept:	
Rate of change:	
Cost for the gym after 2 years?	

3) The population of a town is doubling in size every 5 years after the year 2010. The population was 13,467 in 2010.

Function type:	
Function:	
x-intercept:	
y-intercept:	
Ratio:	
What is the predicted population in 2025?	

4) A rocket is launched from a 30 foot building. The rocket reached its maximum height of 80 feet in 2 seconds.

Function type:	
Function:	
y-intercept:	
Rockets height in 1 second?	

5)

x	0	1	2	3
y	100	50	25	12.5

Function type:	
Function:	
y-intercept:	
Ratio:	

6)

x	1	2	3	4
y	-8	−12	−16	-20

Function type:	
Function:	
x-intercept:	
y-intercept:	
Rate of change:	

7)

x	0	1	2	3
y	10	12	10	4

Function type:	
Function:	
x-intercept:	
y-intercept:	
vertex:	

8)

x	1	2	3	4
y	3	9	27	81

Function type:	
Function:	
x-intercept:	
y-intercept:	
Ratio:	

 # TEST TIME!

Match the graph with the correct Function:

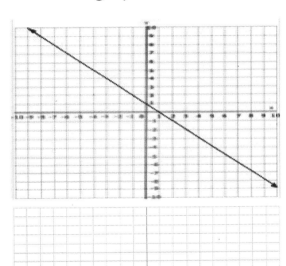

Quadratic
Linear
Exponential

Unit 10 Lesson 6: Average Rate of Change

MA.912.AR.1.1: Identify and interpret parts of an equation or expression that represent a quantity in terms of a mathematical or real-world context, including viewing one or more of its parts as a single entity.

MA.912.F.1.1: Given an equation or graph that defines a function, determine the function type. Given an input-output table, determine a function type that could represent it.

MA.912.F.1.6: Compare key features of linear and nonlinear functions each represented algebraically, graphically, in tables or written descriptions.

MA.912.F.1.8: Determine whether a linear, quadratic or exponential function best models a given real-world situation.

MA.912.F.1.3: Calculate and interpret the average rate of change of a real-world situation represented graphically, algebraically or in a table over a specified interval.

 SHOW US WHAT YOU KNOW!

Write the equation for the table in standard form:

x	y
25	53
26	58
28	68
29	73
30	78

BRAIN WORKOUT!

RATE OF CHANGE:

Rate of change	$m = \dfrac{y_2 - y_1}{x_2 - x_1}$

Find the rate of change and interpret the rate of change.

1)Population of a city is represented in the table.

Year	Population
2000	13,252
2001	15,678
2002	16,230
2003	19,674
2004	18,432
2005	20,177

Rate of change from 2000 to 2002?	Interpret the rate of change:
Rate of change from 2003 to 2004?	Interpret the rate of change:

What is the difference between the rate of change between 2000-2002 and 2003-2004?

2) Given $y = -\frac{1}{2}x^2 + 3x + 5$, where x represents seconds and y represents the height of a rocket in feet.

Average rate of change from 3 seconds to 5 seconds?	Interpret the Average rate of change from 3 seconds to 5 seconds:
Average rate of change from 0 seconds to 3 seconds?	Interpret the Average rate of change from 0 seconds to 3 seconds:

What is the difference between the rate of change between 0-3 seconds and 3-5 seconds?

3) Given $f(x) = 20(2)^x$, where x represents years and f(x) represents total money in a bank account.

Average rate of change from 1 year to 3 years?	Interpret the average rate of change from 1 year to 3 years:
Average rate of change from 4 years to 6 years?	Interpret the average rate of change from 4 years to 6 years:

What is the difference between the rate of change between 1-3 years and 4-6 years?

TEST TIME!

Find the average rate of change for each graph, use the points provided:

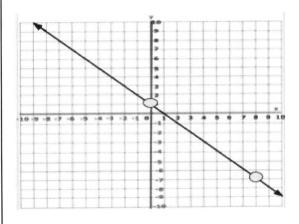

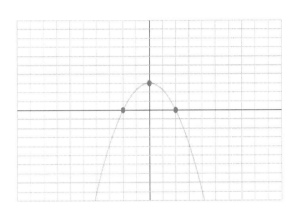

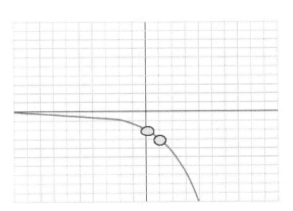

Made in United States
Orlando, FL
16 April 2025

60569338R10122